The Enigma of Time

The Enigma of Time

The last great puzzle of the universe

Editor: Peter Brookesmith

Orbis Publishing · London

Acknowledgments
Photographs were supplied by Aldus Archive, K.M.
Andrew, Associated Press, BBC Hulton Picture Library,
BBC Television, Margaret Baker, John Bethell, The Bowen
Company, Bridgeman Art Library, Bruce Coleman, Country
Life, Robert Cundy Associates, Daily Telegraph, The Dali
Institute/St Petersburg Florida/© by ADAGP Paris 1981,
J.B. Deloir, Department of the Environment, J. Dowding/
Focus, ET Archive, Robert Estall, Mary Evans Picture
Library, Faber and Faber, Robyn Fairweather, Vivien
Fifield, Fitzwilliam Museum, Al Flowerdew, Fortean
Picture Library, French Government Tourist Office, Eileen
Garrett, Ivan Gould, Hale Observatories, Michael Holford,
Robert Hunt Library, Imperial War Museum, Juliette John,
Kobal Collection, Lawrence LeShan, MARS, H. Maddock,
Mansell Collection, NASA, National Monuments Record,
National Portrait Gallery, Photri, Popperfoto, The Press
Agency, Press Association, Psychic News, Rex Features,
Science Photo Library, Soldier Magazine, Spectrum Colour
Library, Suddeutscher Verlag, Syndication International,
David Towersey, David Turner, UKAEA, UPI, Vautier-De
Nauxe, Verulamium Museum/St Albans.

Consultants to
The Unexplained
Professor A.J. Ellinson
Dr J. Allen Hynek
Brian Inglis
Colin Wilson
Editorial Director
Brian Innes
Editor
Peter Brookesmith
Deputy Editor
Lynn Picknett
Executive Editor
Lesley Riley
Sub Editors
Mitzi Bales
Chris Cooper
Jenny Dawson
Hildi Hawkins

Picture Researchers
Anne Horton
Paul Snelgrove
Frances Vargo
Editorial Manager
Clare Byatt
Art Editor
Stephen Westcott
Designer
Richard Burgess
Art Buyer
Jean Morley
Production Co-ordinator
Nicky Bowden
Volume Editors
Lorrie Mack
Francis Ritter

First published in the United Kingdom by
Orbis Publishing Limited, London

Marketed in the United States of America by
Jilli Jay Enterprises Inc., Garnerville,
New York 10923, U.S.A.

Material in this publication previously
appeared in the weekly partwork
The Unexplained, © 1980–83

Printed and bound in Yugoslavia by Gorenjski Tisk, Kranj

Contents

Introduction

THERE IS AN OLD RIDDLE that tells us something about the peculiar way in which we perceive time. A man jumps into the air. But *when* does the 'jumping' take place? Are his feet on the ground, or in the air, when he jumps? Not on the ground, obviously: that's where they were before he jumped. And not in the air, either: that is their position after he's jumped. Our sense of time is something like that. The moment that we call the present is so fleeting that it is instantly past, and we can say that something was inevitable only when we are able to look back on it. Whatever we do to safeguard ourselves, the future is always crammed with pitfalls and remains remorselessly invisible and inscrutable. Yet the past is not much safer, when it comes down to it. Our only access to the past is through memory or imagination – and how many of us agree exactly on what happened yesterday, or on what one person really said to another? Historians spend a vast proportion of their time and energy disagreeing with each other – not because their sources are necessarily different, but because the individual imagination constructs a picture of the past in an idiosyncratic way, and no particular interpretation is bound, *a priori*, to be right.

The answer to the historians' dream would, of course, be the time machine – always assuming that this device wouldn't merely double the acrimony and disputation that graces their discourse. Such a machine would also be a gift to stock-brokers, gamblers, fashion designers and military planners. With this last we are suddenly reminded once again that one man's rosy future is another's nightmare, and it would be something of a miracle of another sort if someone cruising down the centuries in such a contraption weren't tempted – not to say positively *driven* – to change a detail here and there, and tamper with the course of history. Hitler in a time machine? Joseph Stalin? One trembles at the thought.

Perhaps, then, it is fortunate that time *is* like a prison, even though we may on occasion be desperate to find ways to kill it – and all of us know the days we would relive – time and again! – given the chance, and the days too that we would wish changed for ever. To travel in time would also confer a kind of immortality on human beings, as Kurt Vonnegut's hero in *Slaughterhouse five*, Billy Pilgrim, realises when he is given the ability to relive any portion of his life that he chooses. Pilgrim does not, in the event, lose his humanity – by changing the day or the circumstances of his death, for example, or (against the advice of those who gave him the power) by revisiting only the good times he has known. Instead, he uses his travels to ponder the mystery of man's inhumanity, returning again and again to the destruction of Dresden. Although he is not tempted to escape his human fate or his moral sense, Pilgrim's story brings out in stark relief one of the central compulsions that lie behind mankind's fascination – and frustration – with the nature of time: the unavoidable fact of our own individual death, and the fact that none of us has any idea, nor *can* we have any idea, of when it will befall us. (Hence the old, ironic admonition of the rabbis, to be found in the Talmud: 'Repent the day before you die.')

It is a peculiarly obtuse person indeed who is not intrigued by reports that people have, apparently, travelled in time, finding themselves in shops that no longer exist, and even buying things there; or arriving in the midst of a battle that was fought centuries ago. If the immediate reaction to stories of that kind is to say 'It's all an hallucination' and leave the argument there, surely that is to miss the point that one of the curious properties of time is that it is in *any* case experienced subjectively. We know that time can drag, and it can also slip away without our noticing it, if we're sufficiently absorbed in what we're doing. Time is strangely elastic, even within our limited understanding of it, so that to call the experience of slipping from one era to another an hallucination merely begs more questions. To all intents and purposes such an experience is entirely real. In attempting to explain what has 'really' happened we have to acknowledge that we have the choice between dismissing the event as somehow false, or forcing ourselves to speculate about the nature of this most incomprehensible of dimensions. Certainly we have to do the latter in dealing with those rare cases in which similar experiences have occurred to different people at the same time, or at the same place on different occasions.

The very first question that arises here is an old one for psychical researchers: whether we are dealing with a property of the place (the classic instance is the haunted house) or with a property of the individual who witnesses such an occurrence (the psychic phenomenon most commonly associated with particular people is probably the poltergeist). This problem may be quite swiftly solved if the recipient of the timeslip has had similar experiences before, or if a number of people have had a timeslip in the place in question.

For reasons that are still a mystery to researchers, there are certain locations, known as 'window areas', where people become particularly susceptible to paranormal phenomena. Reports include the sighting of UFOs and disturbing timeslip experiences, where the subject finds himself locked in an episode of the location's past, or even its future. Ancient sites, such as Stonehenge in Wiltshire (right), often coincide with window areas, and it has been suggested that some of the monuments we see today were originally positioned in recognition of the sites' strange properties

But this still leaves us with the difficult matter of explaining *how* these connections are taking place across time – sometimes across many generations and many hundreds of years. The channel for the connection may lie in the locality or in an individual percipient, or even both, but the mechanism for what is occurring still defies common sense.

On the other hand, so do modern notions of time and how it works. But these may help us explain what is occurring in a timeslip – and, indeed, in other psychic phenomena as well. The great change in our ideas about time came with Albert Einstein's formulation of his relativity theory. In this, Einstein proposed that the speed of light is a constant, from whatever vantage point it is viewed. Thus, you can travel *towards* a source of light at any speed, and the light will still appear to be approaching you at roughly 186,000 miles per second (300,000 km/sec). Similarly, you can do your best to flee a source of light, and the speed of light relative to you would be unchanged. Thus, according to relativity, time and space are intertwined in some way, and they form a single four-dimensional entity known as 'space-time'. When you move from one place to another, you also move through time. This may sound trite until we remember that in common sense terms it is *time* that does the moving, that 'goes by', not us. In the theory of relativity, Western science agreed with the Zen Buddhist proposition that, contrary to common sense, time is still: it is we who move through it.

With this idea of time before them, physicists found it possible to understand some of the behaviour of the infinitesimally tiny particles that make up the structure of the atom. Electrons change orbits – they shift in space – without appearing to take any time to do so. Their opposite is the positron, which has the same mass as an electron but the opposite electrical charge. If the two meet, they are annihilated. Mathematically it can be shown that if an electron could move backward in time, it would behave just as a positron does. The logical, if astonishing, conclusion is that a positron *is* an electron moving backward in time. And since time travel, in this sense, can occur at the sub-atomic level, in the physical world, there seems to be no reason why the human mind cannot, by some means, do the same.

Another approach to the question of those psychic phenomena that involve apparent travel in time has come from the theory of morphogenesis proposed by Dr Rupert Sheldrake. The theory was originally conceived as an attempt to deal with a problem that biologists and geneticists have so far conspicuously failed to solve: how it is that different species reproduce their enormous variety of forms. The conventional argument that a cat's specific and characteristic shape is somewhere encoded in the animal's genes, although our present state of knowledge cannot tell us precisely how, does not hold water, according to Dr Sheldrake. He suggests instead that the characteristic form of any entity, from a salt crystal to a human embryo, is dictated by a 'morphogenetic field' that is specific to that entity's type. Similar in concept to a magnetic field, the morphogenetic field spans both time and space, carrying information 'transmitted' by 'ancestors' of the entity to the 'receiving' entity in the present, and on into the future. Indeed, this field could be regarded as the connecting link between one time and another – or, in the terms of relativity theory and space-time, between one point *on* time and another. Memory is thus a communication, by means of the morphogenetic field, with the past. A timeslip, in that case, is indeed a subjective experience, but no less real for that – no less real, say, than a telephone conversation that is secure from eavesdroppers.

On its own, this theory does not tell us any more than we already knew about time itself. But it may explain how we manage to communicate *across* time. And it may be worth pointing out here that a memory is itself a form of dwelling in another time. The major question that arises from this argument is that if time is an aspect of space, why is it that we seem unable to communicate normally with the future – since, if time is in some sense static, the future must also be static, fully formed, and merely awaiting our presence.

Resolving this question, at least in theory, not only involves yet another shock for the common sense view of time, it also helps explain the paradox in which, for example, a person may have a precognition of a disaster and is able because of that forewarning to avert it. The paradox is that the precognition is supposed to be a glimpse of the future – yet it is also the agent for changing the future and thus, seemingly, falsifies the precognition.

The paradox is resolved if we think of time as infinitely branching – of time, in other words, as *itself* consisting of two dimensions. Each branch represents the potential development of each particular moment – and each moment is thus the sum of all probabilities. A time-line exists, therefore, for every probable – perhaps every *possible* – action. On one such line the disaster foreseen by the psychic does indeed occur; but the action undertaken to prevent the disaster also exists on another line in time, and that is the one our Universe follows. It has even been suggested that the individual consciousness follows its own time-line, taking the rest of the Universe – its particular Universe – with it. This exactly echoes Sir Arthur Eddington's somewhat cryptic remark that 'The stuff of the world is mind stuff'.

Moreover, this view of time manages to reconcile the idea of free will and the ability to see into the future; it explains why not all precognitions are accurate and furthermore it agrees with relativity that time is an aspect of space, and that the future is, as a dimension if not as a specific and unalterable sequence of events, a fixed entity. Every thing and every action contains the seeds – or the blueprint, as one writer has put it – of the future, although that future is not precisely fixed. This may help explain why the future is less accessible than the past (in the sense that, for instance, we have no 'future memory'): there has been no interplay between possibility and action and therefore it has not yet been fixed in our particular line of time.

Our major problem in understanding time is that our assumptions about its nature, even when backed by mathematics, inevitably remain speculations as long as we ourselves are unable to move freely about, backward and forward, on our own time-lines. Even disregarding this central problem, the subject of time has many other problems associated with it.

One is the question of *why* people find themselves experiencing timeslips: *how* is it that they find themselves dislocated in this way? One suggestion is that there are certain areas on the Earth's surface, sometimes called 'window areas', where people are peculiarly susceptible to paranormal phenomena. The reason for this may lie in certain electrical disturbances associated with the place (which is not to say that the electrical disturbances themselves are not a symptom rather than a cause of the peculiarity of the places in question). The renowned dowser Tom Lethbridge was convinced that the presence of water had some connection with paranormal phenomena. Other researchers point to anomalies in local magnetic conditions as a possible stimulus to such events. As cynics might point out, this in turn may be merely a convenient hypothesis, if only because science is not certain about the nature of that particular beast either.

Or perhaps there are less obvious, less materialistic, explanations of timeslip experiences: a combination of gesture, mood, and circumstance may echo the past in such a way as to usher the unsuspecting percipient into another era, as though two mismatched but perfectly fitting pieces of jigsaw were accidentally locked together for a while. But even if we were to discover why people find themselves slipping in time (and there is no reason yet to suppose that there is only one true explanation – any more than there is for a car breaking down on the highway), we could still be none the wiser about the mechanism that *allows* this to happen. It would be rather like finding a key without knowing which door it fitted or how locks work. And this is because we cannot stand aside from time in order to examine it. Our understanding remains trapped in our circumstances – our inability to stop ourselves forging through time as if we were tied to the front of a runaway locomotive.

That is not to say that time, as such, cannot be slowed down: indeed, our own journey through time can, in theory, be made to decelerate. This proposition is perfectly respectable, but to carry it out in practice requires us to get within spitting distance of a black hole – which isn't, yet, within the means of most of us. Nonetheless, were anyone able to sit in the gravitational field of a black hole, he or she *would* take longer to age than anyone on the outside. There are two major disadvantages to this programme, however: anyone in such a position will find the Universe speeding up, rather than life getting longer; and, perhaps more to the point, once someone is *in* that gravitational field, it is impossible for him to get back out. This means that the ability to see everyone else's future is of no personal advantage, and certainly of no advantage to anyone else, since it is still not possible to go 'back' in time to announce the next day's news. On the other hand, this argument may be based on one vast fallacy: for if the notion of a time that constantly branches is true, time travel forward or backward is irrelevant: we need to learn how to travel sideways, not *in time* but *across times* – from one universe to another. And there is indeed a proposal from one respected physicist that this movement would not only be consistent with the theory of relativity but it should, given the resources, be a practical proposition. In other words, a time machine could be built after all.

This somewhat astonishing feat would depend simply on the provision an enormous object rotating in space with the proper combinations of mass, density and angular velocity to provide a region of warped space-time from which it is possible to escape. All the intrepid time traveller then needs to do is move into this warped region, head in the direction of negative time, and take himself back to Earth: he will then find that he has moved into the past. To come back to his original starting point in time, he simply reverses the process. None of this offends against any known physical law, although putting it into practice may well offend someone's sense of economic priorities.

For to create such a time machine probably requires at the very least the means to reach the nearest pulsar (a star of sufficient density and speed of rotation to provide the raw material for the job) and then to sculpt it into the required shape. This, it will be readily agreed, is not a task for amateurs, and not even one for impecunious professionals.

Even if the will and the resources were available for such a project, however, a couple of problems remain. One is that the time machine thus created cannot take a traveller back in time any further than the moment of its own creation, so many generations would have to pass before it could be usefully used as a research tool for historians. It could, on the other hand, be used to inspect the future – a possibility that raises the questions we have already discussed about *which* future – which universe, indeed – the time traveller would find himself visiting. The other difficulty, which we also touched on earlier, has to do with questions of cause and effect that arise once one arrives in an area of the past, and then is able to do something that radically affects the time in which one normally lives.

For instance, it is conceivable that someone would take it into his head to visit the Germany of the early 1920s and make certain that in the street fighting following Hitler's attempted *putsch* in Munich, the budding Nazi leader was killed. It's a reasonable supposition that, without his charisma, the Nazi movement would not have achieved power and that the millions who died would have lived; and thus Europe would be a very different place today. To which future would this time traveller return? The one that results from his admirable assassination of Hitler, or the one from which he has travelled? And which one is real? (After all, the future that excludes Hitler may also, in its fundamentally altered state, exclude *him* too.) Only the idea that 'loops' may exist in time, or that universes may exist in parallel, can accommodate this problem; and yet the question still remains: what was the point of the good deed if, in another time or universe, those millions still continue to suffer?

One man who speculated on the nature of time may have hit upon the answer to difficulties like these. J.B. Priestley suggested in his book *Man and time* that there are three kinds of time: clock time, the possible future, and time as it exists in the creative imagination. Clock time is a necessary fiction, says Priestley, to explain why events seem to follow one another, and it is from this that we – falsely – derive the idea of cause and effect. Take away clock time and not only is time seen to follow whatever whimsy it likes, but one particular kind of common experience begins to make sense, involving as it does the notion of imagination as an aspect of time.

I am thinking here of the shock that everyone has had at one time or another in realising that the drift or meaning of past events has been utterly different from the way it appeared when those events occurred. Motives and intentions are revealed for what they really were; insignificant behaviour acquires a new, different and real significance. Much writing, from the unpretentious detective novel to some of the most highly wrought works of literature, depends on this clash between present appearance and ultimate reality. It is perhaps not insignificant that they are, if anything is, works of the creative imagination. They are aspects of time.

Modern science has provided some startling insights into the nature of time – or, to put it another way, science has persisted in making claims about time that were once the province of the imagination alone. An awareness of both time and human creativity is central to making any sense at all of our existence. Both, paradoxically and perhaps necessarily, are things we take for granted, and yet they remain essentially mysterious and perplexing.   PETER BROOKESMITH

There seems to be no limit to how far a person's awareness can travel in time. JOAN FORMAN examines long-term timeslips and discusses some cases in which witnesses seemed to experience events from times long before their own birth

TIMESLIPS – THE BAFFLING INTRUSIONS of the events of one time into those of another – show an extraordinary range in the degree of dislocation involved. In a timeslip into the future there may be only a few minutes between a precognitive experience and the event that it anticipates, or there may be a delay of many years – perhaps centuries. Sometimes the experiences relate to events seemingly so far in the future that a date cannot be put on them. An equally wide variation is found in timeslips into the past.

The onset of a timeslip is always sudden. The only warning a subject may experience is a faint tingling on the skin or a sensation of nausea, similar to that which some people feel before a thunderstorm or earthquake. Other people are swept into the timeslip without warning, however. Such was the case of an English woman, Mrs M. Rawlings of Barnet in north London. She 'saw' a Roman procession entering the arena at Verulamium (modern St Albans). She noted the uniformed rank and file soldiers and the standard-bearers carrying the eagle insignia. Last of all came a high-ranking official dressed in white and wearing a laurel wreath. He sat down in a chair in the centre of the

The Roman theatre at Verulamium – now the English city of St Albans – must have seen many splendid ceremonial occasions in its heyday (below). Such an event seems to have been 'seen' by a modern woman among the present-day ruins (bottom)

platform, with a standard-bearer taking up position on each side of him. The experience ended at that point. Mrs Rawlings had witnessed a scene that could easily have taken place in Verulamium some 19 centuries earlier.

The Romans made a deep impression in British consciousness and many of the truly long-distance timeslips relate to events connected with their occupation. Often these replayed fragments of Romano-British history bear a strong resemblance to the traditional haunting. Indeed the dividing line between some timeslips into the past and certain types of haunting is a shadowy one.

An example of such a borderline case is

A step through time

A detachment of the Roman army seems to have returned to the English cathedral city of York – called Eboracum in Roman times – more than 15 centuries after they had left it. A heating engineer, Harry Martindale, was working on some pipes in a cellar of the medieval Treasurer's House (right) when he heard a trumpet call. In terror he watched as a figure wearing a 'kilt' and carrying a round shield marched through one wall. It was followed by an officer on horseback and then a column of about 14 or 16 unkempt and dispirited men. Martindale cowered in one corner as they marched diagonally across the cellar and vanished through the far wall.

Most remarkable of all, the men marched thigh-deep in the floor of the cellar. He glimpsed their feet only where they passed through a hole dug in the floor. Martindale believed they were marching on the old Roman road, now buried.

Martindale's mention of round shields, which Roman soldiers did not use, caused puzzlement at the time. Later it was found that the Sixth Legion, based at York, had been strengthened with auxiliaries – with round shields.

the incident at Oldbury Camp in Wiltshire, southern England, in which a shepherd saw a detachment of Roman soldiers on the march. Another is the apparition of a dishevelled band of Romans seen marching through a York cellar.

These three cases have a common factor: each concerns Roman military activity. The legions led a highly organised life of routine and regularity, and this seems to favour the paranormal 'recording' of events. The similarly disciplined life of monasteries and convents also seems to have left traces in numerous haunted sites.

Another paranormal 'record' left from the period of Roman rule in Britain may be mentioned here: the 'Cammeringham light'. Cammeringham is a small village near Lincoln in north-east England. It lies not far from Ermine Street, an old Roman road. A Mr Lucas was walking to work early one misty morning when he noticed large banks of vapour forming ahead of him – a not unusual occurrence at the beginning of a warm day. For no special reason Lucas found himself watching a particularly large bank of mist drifting towards him. Then a chariot emerged from it, driven by a woman and pulled by two horses, one black and one white. The woman wore a long flowing dress and her hair lay loose upon her shoulders. She whipped up the horses and Lucas saw the flash of gold jewellery as the early sunlight caught it. Almost immediately the chariot was swallowed again in the mist. Only then did the observer realise that he had

heard no sound throughout the experience. He was convinced he had seen Boudicca, Queen of the Iceni – and the Icenian territories did indeed run well up into south Lincolnshire. This apparition – called the 'Cammeringham light' because of a curious hazy quality in the appearance of the figure – has been witnessed several times over the centuries.

Such echoes of the far-distant past do not always involve human figures, however. Occasionally long-vanished scenery appears. Only diligent research can establish that it belongs to the place where it is seen. There are cases of buildings reappearing on their old sites many years after their demolition. Natural features of the countryside can also reappear, as in the timeslip that occurred to a woman driving alongside the river Tweed in the Scottish border country.

A large area of this beautiful valley is administered by the Forestry Commission. But at the time of this experience they had not begun their planting. Since the 15th century the valley had been farming country: sheep and cattle were grazed there and provided a target for hungry raiders from both sides of the border. So at the time of this drive, from Moffat to Edinburgh, the valley would have been open, rolling hill country, with a certain amount of woodland. But the woman in fact drove through a great forest of tall trees, composed, as far as she could tell, of Scots fir, ash and oak – which made up the ancient indigenous forests of Scotland. The later afforestation is quite different, for it consists of spruce, pine and larch.

The Romans had reached this area; they built a signalling station outside Moffat, at the great hollow called the Devil's Beef Tub. Although no Roman road was ever built along the Tweed Valley, an ancient track once ran there. It may be that the modern road picks up its course for a while – and sometimes the memories associated with it.

Sometimes the persons involved in a long-term timeslip find that they themselves seem to have changed physically – not necessarily in their own bodily form, but in their dress, appearance and demeanour. Such a change is often extremely upsetting to the person concerned, bringing with it the disturbing sense of being in two times at once and afterwards prompting thoughts of previous incarnations.

This happened to Mrs Phyllis Hester, who, while standing by a table in the old hall of St William's College in the ancient English cathedral city of York, felt herself to be dressed in a long robe and to be at a much earlier time in the building's history. She was surprised when she came out of her reverie and found herself in her modern short dress.

An echo from a more recent era, though one still separated from the present by more than a century, came to Mrs C. Maddison as she travelled in a bus in southern England. It was February, the weather was bitterly cold and snow was falling when, dressed in boots, trousers and a heavy coat, she set out on her journey. As she sat in the moving bus she was overcome by what, in her later account, she

described as a 'peculiar feeling':

> I no longer had trousers, coat and boots on, but a bonnet, cape and long dress. If I rubbed my hands together I could feel the silk from my skirt. I jerked myself back to reality and stared out at the snow-covered roofs; then it started again – jolt, jolt, as though I were in a horse-drawn carriage. I started to twist my fingers anxiously and for some reason I felt a great urgency to get somewhere, but where I did not know. On we went and I felt the long ringlets bouncing on my neck.

This brought Mrs Maddison back to the present and she realised that the sensation was caused by her fur hood tickling her neck.

However, the experience was not yet finished. She found that she did not recognise the many small shops in a village that she passed through. 'There were no pavements, only cobblestones, and I suddenly became aware of absolute solitude.' Then the present again returned with a rush. When the vehicle reached a point at which there should be traffic lights, Mrs Maddison saw an old signpost. One arm bore the legend 'St Albanse'. The crossroads were muddy and deeply marked by the tracks of wheeled vehicles – but they were not tyre marks. The phenomenon did not cease until the woman

Left: Boudicca, Queen of the Iceni and a heroine of the English for her resistance to the Roman occupation. At long intervals she is apparently seen in an apparition called the 'Cammeringham light', which appears in Lincolnshire

Below left: the Devil's Beef Tub, a large natural depression near Moffat in Dumfriesshire, near the Scottish border. Marked today by this memorial to a 17th-century religious martyr, it was the site of a Roman signalling station. An apparent timeslip experienced by a woman driving near here may, like so many similar occurrences, have been associated with the Roman occupation

alighted at her destination.

To apprehend the present more or less simultaneously with the past or future in this way is highly unusual. The woman felt a strong identification with the Victorian woman whose attributes she had apparently taken on, and the incident made a profound impression on her.

Here is another incident in which those involved not only perceived another time but actually took part in events occurring in it. During the Second World War Mrs B.W. McDougall, who was in the Women's Auxiliary Air Force, was travelling with two friends to the RAF station at Abingdon in southern England. They did not know the

Above: St William's College, York, founded in 1453, was originally a college for priests. While visiting the building Mrs Phyllis Hester had the sensation of being a woman of some century past, in a long robe

Below: Richard II personally confronts the rebels during the Peasants' Revolt of 1381. During the Second World War an airwoman seemed to experience an incident from this rebellion

area at all, having never previously visited it. They were therefore disconcerted to find they had missed the transport sent to meet them. Rural England at midnight in December and in the wartime blackout was not the happiest place to be. They had no choice but to walk to the camp.

Having lost their way they found themselves approaching a bridge. The night was cold and showery, so there was no thought in their minds as they passed under the bridge except to get to camp as soon as possible. The moment they were beneath the bridge Mrs McDougall felt the situation change. She seemed to be transported into another time – the time of the Peasants' Revolt, in the 14th century:

> I was one of a crowd of people scurrying under the bridge getting out of the way of trouble. It was hot, I smelt the sweat, and felt the heat of bodies pressing close to mine. I also felt the roughness of coarse cloth and knew my heart was beating with fright. I was conscious of heavy coarse cloth trailing at my feet, and had a feeling of dread and unease.

As soon as she emerged from the bridge she found herself back in the present. The interlude had lasted only a few seconds, but its impression was vivid and lasting.

Disturbances may very well have occurred in the Abingdon area during the Peasants' Revolt, but whether the incident described by the witness ever occurred in reality is not known. But while it lasted the 20th-century girl felt herself to be a 14th-century woman.

Timeslips into the future are even more disturbing than timeslips into the past – for they suggest that our lives are fixed in advance. This chapter describes some striking examples of such excursions into the future

PRECOGNITION MUST SURELY BE the strangest kind of disruption of our time experience. Sometimes it is short-term, and only a few minutes, days or weeks elapse between the experience and the events that bear it out. But sometimes 20 years or more can pass between foresight and fulfilment. On occasion, the precognition is forgotten until the events foreseen actually occur.

Following a series of television programmes on the subject of timeslips, an English clergyman wrote to the BBC describing three precognitive dreams that he had experienced during one period of his life. They had occurred in the space of two months in about 1965 when he was vicar of a parish in Nottinghamshire.

Each dream began in the same way, in a vicarage that he recognised as being his childhood home. Yet in each dream the house seemed to belong to a different church. In the first he left the vicarage to inspect the church: it was a beautiful medieval one. In the second dream the church was a large and dark Victorian building. The third dream included a variation, for the dreamer did not walk from the vicarage to the church, but walked to the bottom of the garden before seeing what he took to be the ruins of Hadleigh Castle, near Benfleet in Essex.

The clergyman forgot his dreams and did not recall them until he was appointed to his next parish, at Saxmundham in Suffolk. Its medieval church precisely matched the church that had appeared in his first dream the previous year.

Five years passed before the clergyman's next change of residence. He had dismissed the possibility that the second dream would be fulfilled, for he did not care for Victorian churches and thought it unlikely that he would accept an appointment to one. Yet when in 1971 he was offered a living in Beckenham, Kent, he accepted it at once,

The medieval church at Saxmundham in the East Anglian county of Suffolk. In 1966 a new incumbent arrived in this parish – and recognised the church as the one that he had seen in the first of a series of dreams in the previous year

Future shock

only later realising that its large Victorian church was the one he had seen in the dream.

By now both he and his wife were impressed by the accuracy of the dreams. But they had to wait until 1977 to test the truth of the third. It was then that the clergyman was appointed vicar of St Mary's, Bury St Edmunds, in Suffolk. He discovered that at the bottom of the very large churchyard were the ruins of an old abbey. There two sections of wall rose – and they resembled remarkably closely the two towers of Hadleigh Castle.

The clergyman was certain that he did not allow his dreams to influence his acceptance of any of the livings. He recollected the dream prophecies only when he had actually accepted the appointments and moved into the respective vicarages.

Landscape of fear

There was a lapse of 12 years between the clergyman's third dream and its fulfilment. An even greater length of time was spanned by a recurrent precognitive dream that first occurred in 1955. The setting of the dream, which was experienced by a married English woman, was always the same: a flat landscape of fields with a windmill in the distance, the whole scene enclosed by leafless trees and a hedge. The action of the dream was also basically the same in each repetition: she was always running through grass and mud towards the windmill, with the sound of feet pounding behind her in pursuit. The mill seemed to be her goal and to represent safety – but she never succeeded in reaching it.

As often happens in recurrent dreams, the action developed with time. No longer did she merely hear the sounds of pursuit, she actually came to see the pursuer's shadow on the grass and she knew that whoever or whatever was chasing her was gaining ground. The dream was frightening and verged on nightmare. Although in the dream she was never caught by her pursuer, neither did she escape or find help.

In 1970 the woman and her husband moved to East Anglia. Although the landscape around their home at Sutton, in Norfolk, was flat and agricultural, the woman did not connect it with her dream.

Shortly after their move the husband died. And only then did the wife discover the landscape of her dream. She had often seen the Sutton windmill but not from an angle where she could have identified it with the windmill in the dream. Not, that is, until the usual road to the mill was being repaired, and the woman found herself obliged to approach the mill from its far side. At once she found herself in the dream landscape – the waving grass, ploughed field, bare trees and the windmill itself, at the angle at which she had always seen it in the dream. The dream had always had a winter setting; the woman's husband had died in January.

Subsequently this woman came to feel

Below: abbey ruins at Bury St Edmunds in Suffolk, East Anglia. This is another site that the clergyman seems to have seen in one of his precognitive dreams. He took the ruins in his dream to be those of Hadleigh Castle in Essex – until he encountered the abbey ruins

Left: the magnificent church of St Mary's at Bury St Edmunds, dating from the 15th century. It was fully 12 years after the last of his series of timeslip dreams that the clergyman took up the living at this church – and fulfilled the precognition

that the pursuer in her dream was death – or, at least, the disaster represented by the loss of her husband. After his death the dream did not recur. There had been about 15 years between its first occurrence and the woman's recognition of the dream landscape.

Could the dreamer have gained her knowledge of the mill from her subconscious memory? Although she had never visited Norfolk when she began to have the dreams it is possible that at some time she had seen a picture of the Sutton mill and then forgotten it. But it is surely stretching credulity too far to suggest that it was pure coincidence that, years later, she should move to live beside that very mill; and that it was coincidence that she should experience the threat and fear of bereavement in the place where, in her dream, she had felt just such emotions.

Two-level timeslip

Here is another example of one of these strange, chilling and almost inexplicable long-term precognitions.

In 1896 a small boy in Hanley, Staffordshire, in the English Midlands, was given a severe beating by a sadistic schoolmaster for some minor misdemeanour. The child was very young – seven years old – and sensitive.

> Instead of going to school in the afternoon I played truant. I remember even now running along the street scraping my iron-shod boots on the pavement so as to strike sparks. Also stopping to listen to organ music coming from a little church although the church was empty and locked up. Across the road at the end of the street there was (and still is) an archway to a street running at right-angles. It led to the backs of the houses and shops. To the left it was very short as there were only two (I think) houses, and it was terminated by a blank wall. At the other side of the wall there was a vast area of waste land.

> On this particular day there was a doorway in the wall and when I went through I found myself in a different world, a small town with houses nothing like any I had ever seen before. I went along one street and all the houses were empty. I entered several but came out again without attempting any exploration. Eventually I stayed in one of the houses and going upstairs I came to a large room looking on to a landscape I had never seen before. The land sloped away to a valley, although I could not see what was at the bottom, and beyond there were low tree-covered hills. Even at that age I was fascinated by the sun and the stars and I realised that I was facing east.

> That was the vision. What my physical body was doing I haven't the least idea and I can't think of one; most certainly an adventurous boy of seven

The windmill at Sutton in Norfolk, East Anglia. A woman who had newly moved to this district recognised the windmill and the surroundings as those she had seen in a recurrent dream that she had first had 15 years previously. The dream had been filled with fear inspired by an unseen pursuer; her first view of the windmill in reality occurred at a time when she was still suffering from the shock of her husband's death

would not play truant just to go to sleep.

These recollections were described many decades later, when the subject of the experiences had retired from a career as a professor of electrical engineering. The events that the 'vision' anticipated occurred during the First World War:

> Early in 1917 the Germans broke off the Somme battles and made a retirement of about forty miles [65 kilometres]. Besides taking the High Command completely by surprise they left a desert forty miles [65 kilometres] wide.

> I was sent to 4th Army Headquarters which was established a little way east of a deserted village called Villers Carbonnel. It was close to the River Somme where it runs northwards before taking an abrupt turn to the west at St Quentin.

> One evening I had some hours free and I decided to explore some of the neighbouring villages and make a few sketches (which I still have). I came to a village called Misery (most appropriately) and when I entered it I had that feeling which is described as hairraising. I was in the street of my earlier vision. All the people were gone, apart

from dead Germans I found in several houses I entered and hurriedly left. Then I found a house free of these unpleasant occupants and going upstairs I found myself in the large room facing east. The landscape was exactly as I had found it before. The valley was the Somme valley but as Misery is some way back the river is not visible.

There was another curious factor. In his childhood 'hallucination' the subject had happened to notice that the village street in which he seemed to find himself was named Windmill Street. When the professor revisited Hanley in about 1960 he found that an estate of houses had been built on the waste ground, beyond the archway he had used that day in 1896. One of its streets was called Windmill Street.

This is one of the most complex and convincing cases of long-distance precognition. Not only did the vision present in great detail the exact scene that the professor was to visit 20 years after his childhood experience; it also presented the street name that would be associated with the site of the experience decades later. It worked, therefore, on two levels: one concerned the personal history of the small boy, 20 years ahead; the other concerned the history of the site of the experience, some 65 years ahead. It would be interesting to know whether there is any Rue du Moulin in the French village of Misery.

The extraordinary and arresting phenomenon of precognition, of seeing the future anything from minutes to years ahead of the

Below: Hanley, part of the industrial city of Stoke-on-Trent in the English Midlands. In 1896 in this area, which was then waste ground, a small boy playing truant found himself apparently in a street named Windmill Street, in a village unlike any he had ever seen. Years later he was to recognise the village in war-stricken France – and decades later still, to find that a Windmill Street now stood on the former waste ground

observer's 'now', can hardly be disputed in the face of evidence that has accumulated throughout the ages. In the cases we have described a comparison could be made between the vision and the events that matched it. Doubtless many precognitions occur that are not sufficiently striking to be remembered in this way and so their validity cannot be subsequently confirmed. But there are also apparent precognitions referring to times so far ahead that their date cannot be guessed at. They appear to transport the subject into an era and an environment that are barely recognisable.

Left: the village of Misery in the valley of the Somme, in western France, as it looked after the German retreat of 1917. This was the village seen by the child in Hanley 21 years before, and recognised by him when he was an officer with the British Army in 1917. In the timeslip experience the village was uninhabited; at the time the officer saw it, its only occupants were the corpses of German soldiers. Was the 'cosmic joker' at work when a vision of Misery came to a child who was *in misery* at the time?

'This is how it will be'

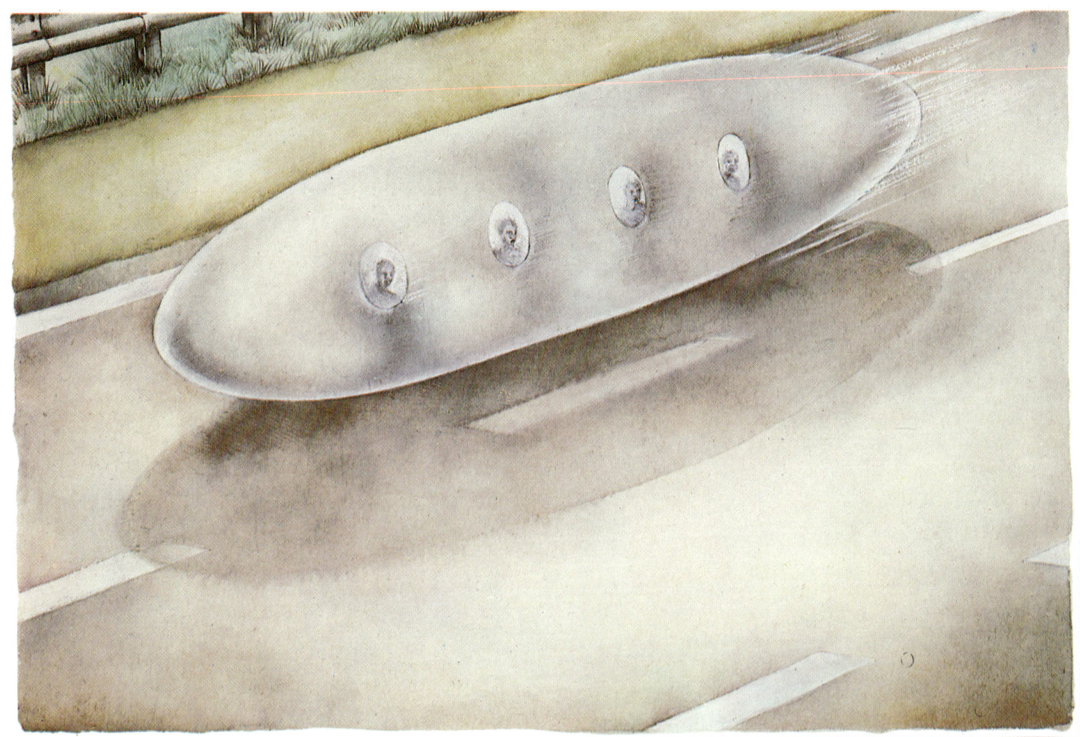

Science fiction writers exert their imaginations to the utmost to portray the far distant future, but many timeslip case histories indicate that some ordinary people have caught glimpses of things the fantasy writers would love to see

MOST PRECOGNITIVE EXPERIENCES relate to events in the near future. A minority seem to 'view' the more distant future – years rather than weeks or months ahead. And a very few belong to a totally different category. They appear to take the subject to a time quite outside his own earthly lifetime, perhaps even centuries ahead. These are the cases that stretch belief to its limits.

One such experience occurred to a British family when on holiday in Germany. They were travelling in their car on one of the motorways. There was nothing particularly noteworthy about the day or the weather conditions, and as far as they could later judge nothing had occurred beforehand to prepare them for the incident.

Presently they became aware of a vehicle approaching them in the opposite carriageway, apparently travelling faster than they were. It was not this that drew their attention, however, so much as the vehicle's shape. It was long and cylindrical, and there were what appeared to be round windows, or portholes, in the side. And out of those windows, looking straight at them, were four

Travelling on one of the motorways that criss-cross Germany (above), a family of British holidaymakers saw an extraordinary apparition – a silvery torpedo-shaped object (top) travelling fast in the opposite carriageway, with frightened faces peering at them through the vehicle's round windows

very frightened faces. Needless to say, the family presented equally alarmed faces at their own car windows!

Afterwards the travellers were unable to liken the machine to anything they had seen before. They do not appear to have observed any wheels on the vehicle, nor were they aware of any engine noise. Had the object been seen in the sky it might have been classified as a UFO. On the ground it looked like a vision of the far-distant future, a machine that was the remote descendant of the modern car. The holidaymakers were, not surprisingly, unnerved.

Another remarkable experience occurred to a London man, a Mr D'Alessio, when he was taking a walk in the tree-lined street in which he lived. The evening was warm and

pleasant, and he walked slowly, enjoying the weather.

It was then that he began to feel, as he described it, 'strange, as if in a dream'. The sensation was not new to him, for he had had similar feelings in the past, and they had invariably preceded some form of time dislocation or out-of-the-body experience.

On this occasion he continued to be perfectly well-aware of who he was and where he was, although he felt that his personality was somewhat different from usual: he was a happier, more relaxed and less tense person. He felt that he was in the same familiar location, but he was also certain that the time was not the present. He seemed to be in the far future. A haze covered the entire scene 'and this haze trembled and stirred quite uniformly.'

He was particularly impressed by the fact that everything was extremely quiet; the traffic in particular made no sound. The conviction came to him that this traffic of the future could move not only in silence but also in complete safety. He felt that 'accidents are no longer possible, because vehicles cannot crash or collide any more.'

Another aspect of the scene struck the witness forcibly: the texture of the road surface and of the dwellings. They were made of the same synthetic substance, 'very smooth and silvery and beneficial to one's well-being'. It seemed to have qualities that no material in our own time has.

Mr D'Alessio continued to stroll along the street, enjoying the sensation and thinking: 'This is how it will be.' After a few minutes the haze faded and both the scene and his

Gilston Road, Fulham – the London street in which a Mr D'Alessio had the conviction that he had suddenly slipped into the future – into a time when the traffic was silent and vehicles could not collide. The road and buildings were made of a smooth and silvery substance. This was one of several time dislocations and out-of-the-body experiences that had occurred in Mr D'Alessio's life

sensations returned to normal. He was left with a feeling of considerable happiness.

Mr D'Alessio regards his timeslips as involuntary and not capable of being produced to order in any circumstances. They are always accompanied by the slightly dreamy, though not sleepy, sensation described. As he says: 'It is as if something strange and yet familiar is about to happen [but] at a different rate.'

This disjointed, 'out of phase' sensation is a common accompaniment of all timeslips, whether into the past or the future. They are also frequently marked by a silvery or hazy light over the scene and by a noticeable absence of sound.

Timeslip in Tombland

A similar incident occurred to an elderly man whom we shall call Mr Raven, who lives in Norfolk, in East Anglia. One day in early autumn he and his wife made one of their rare visits to the county town of Norwich. They spent part of their visit in the central shopping area and then wandered into the district known as Tombland. This was the site of the city's market in medieval times, and is bounded by shops on one side and by the cathedral, and buildings fronting it, on the other. The main street through Tombland is usually crowded with cars and people.

Mr and Mrs Raven found themselves in a narrow side street. The husband left his wife waiting on the pavement while he went to a nearby public toilet. But instead of being away for a few minutes, as he had expected, Mr Raven was away for an hour. The story he told his worried wife when he returned was a strange and troubling one.

He had entered the lavatory, he thought, by a door that opened directly from the street and that was at street level. When he wished to come out he saw another door in a different position from the first, with a flight of steps that led upward – to the street. He took this exit, only to find himself in a street quite different from that which he had left. It was like Tombland – but not the Tombland he had left.

Traffic was streaming along this street in a continuous, unbroken flow, moving so fast that it was quite impossible for a pedestrian to cross the road at any point. There seemed to be few people about and the only form of traffic control was a set of lights flashing alternately red and green without intermission. Warehouses and industrial buildings now stood where the cathedral and its associated buildings had been.

He stood in bewilderment for a long time and then began to wander up and down the nearby streets, trying to find his wife. He has no idea to this day how he did find her; but eventually he found himself in the narrow street that he had left, where he saw his wife, by now very anxious, still waiting for him.

Elements of doubt

Mr Raven felt that he may have seen the distant future of Norwich. But there are certain elements in the story that throw doubt on this explanation of his experience. The first is that the single entrance of the only public lavatory in the Tombland area is not at ground level but is approached by descending steps. In the second place, red and green traffic lights do exist nearby today, in the form of the pedestrian crossing at the top of the hill, about 70 yards (64 metres) away. The traffic lights do not flash red and green but intermittently flash amber, and the pedestrian crossing light flashes green at times.

Nevertheless the inexplicable fact is that Mr Raven did not see the cathedral and its associated buildings, which are present in Tombland today, but did see industrial-style buildings, which are not. The 'lost time' of an hour is puzzling, too, for it would be difficult for Mr Raven to be lost for that length of time in such a small area if he had merely become confused about his whereabouts. And the traffic, though it always moves fast in this area, does not maintain a smooth, unbroken flow. Furthermore the place is usually crowded with pedestrians at that time of day.

How can these long-term timeslips occur? To this question we can proffer only intelligent guesses. In cases where scenes from the past are witnessed by a present-day subject, it may be that some form of recording of an actual event is stored in the physical environment, capable, under the right conditions, of being 'replayed' and 'picked up' by a witness whose brain is properly attuned.

The Erpingham Gate (below) of Norwich Cathedral is one of the conspicuous features of the city's Tombland district. Yet neither it nor any other recognisable landmark could be seen by a timeslip subject, 'Mr Raven', when, on leaving the public lavatory (bottom), he spent an hour wandering – apparently in the distant future. Warehouses stood where familiar buildings should have been, and instead of the clogged traffic of today there was an unbroken, fast-moving stream of vehicles

Or it may be that the memory of some former incarnation is stored in the brain of the modern observer and is evoked by the combination of, say, a particular place, temperature and state of the light.

Precognition does not fit into either of these models. But many scientists do not look on the idea with disfavour. 'In physics, everything that is *not* forbidden occurs. And physics does *not* forbid the transmission of information from the future to the present.' These are physicists speaking, the Americans Harold Puthoff and Russell Targ. The behaviour of subatomic particles suggests that information travelling backwards in time is not unknown.

The author's own theory is that all matter contains the 'blueprint' of its own future, and there are occasions when this pattern superimposes itself on our workaday present. Then we see events from our own future.

Visions of the future beyond our own life span may also be explicable in this way; but in such cases the 'blueprint' must lie in the surroundings and not in the subject, though it is the latter's brain that translates the information into experiences of sounds and images. But how such information is stored and 'replayed' remains a mystery.

Time is one of the concepts about which there seems to be no 'common sense' in the bizarre theories of today. ARCHIE ROY sketches the background to this climate, in which the psychical discoveries of the late 1800s conflicted with the scientific view

THE GREATEST OBSTACLE to acceptance of paranormal events is not the lack of evidence but the firmly entrenched belief that such events are impossible. Many eminent psychical researchers have drawn attention to this phenomenon – and, much to their dismay, have discovered it in themselves. Professor Charles Richet, a renowned physiologist and Nobel laureate, a keen, sceptical and long-term researcher into alleged psychic phenomena, wrote the following after his carefully conducted series of tests of Eusapia Palladino, the famous – some would say notorious – physical medium:

> But at this point a remarkable psychological phenomenon made itself felt; a phenomenon deserving of all your attention. Observe that we are now dealing with observed facts which are nevertheless absurd; which are in contradiction with facts of daily observation; which are denied not by science only, but by the whole of humanity – facts which are rapid and fugitive, which take place in semi-darkness, and almost by surprise; with no proof except the testimony of our senses, which we know to be often fallible.

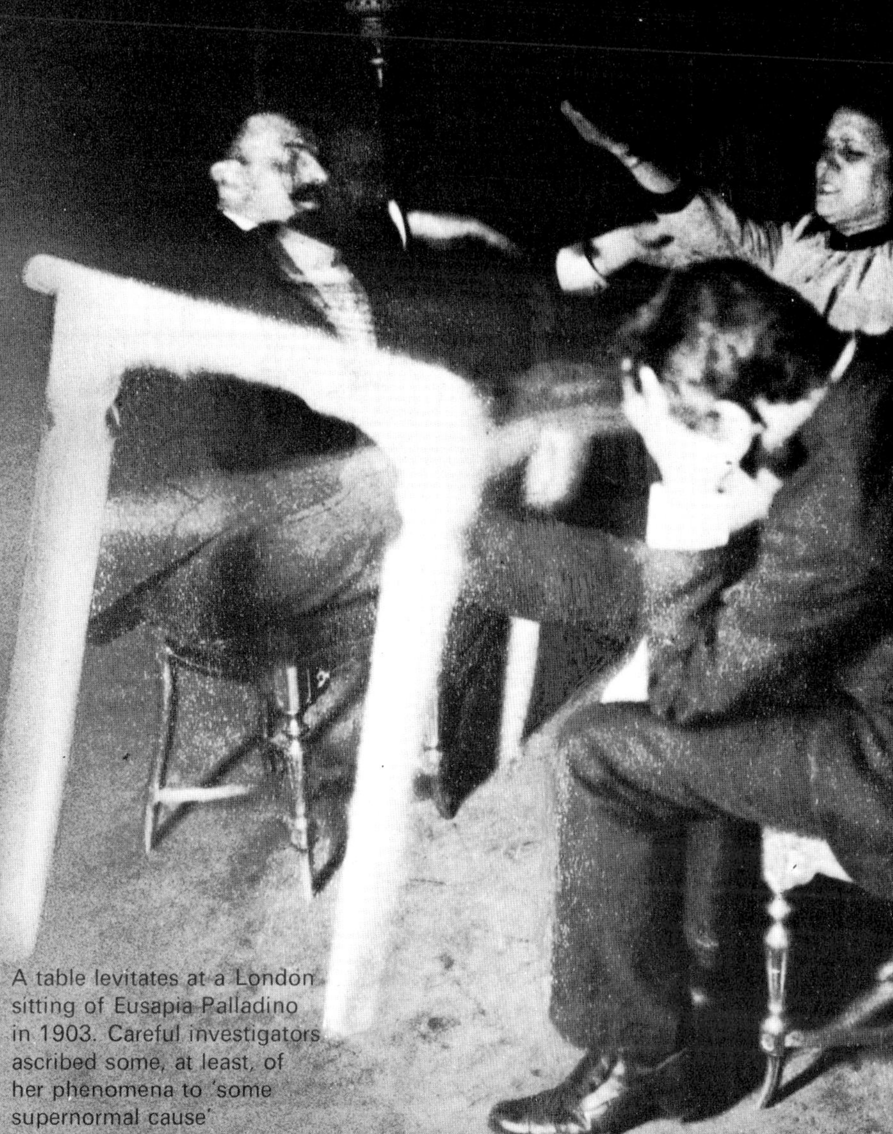

A table levitates at a London sitting of Eusapia Palladino in 1903. Careful investigators ascribed some, at least, of her phenomena to 'some supernormal cause'

Outrageous and unthinkable

> After we have witnessed such facts, everything concurs to make us doubt them. Now, at the moment when these facts take place they seem to us certain, and we are willing to proclaim them openly; but when we return to ourself, when we feel the irresistible influence of our environment, when our friends all laugh at our credulity – then we are almost disarmed, and we begin to doubt. May it not all have been an illusion? May I not have been grossly deceived? . . . And then, as the moment of the experiment becomes more remote, that experiment which once seemed so conclusive gets to seem more and more uncertain, and we end by letting ourselves be persuaded that we have been the victims of a trick.

Everard Feilding, one of the most cautious investigators of the paranormal, also testified to the disorientating effect of prolonged contact with the incredible:

> The effect of all this on my mind was

Charles Richet, a French physiologist, was convinced of Eusapia Palladino's genuineness

> singular. I appeared to lose touch with actualities. Once admit the possibility of such things – and the mere fact of investigating them implied such an admission – where could one stop? I wrote at the time that I gradually began to feel that if a man seriously told me that the statue of the Albert Memorial had called in to tea I should have to admit that the question to be solved would not be the sanity of the narrator but the evidence for the fact.

Walter Franklin Prince, in his book *The enchanted boundary*, wrote of the strange spell psychic phenomena seemed to cast over many respectable men of science: they became so immediately antagonistic to the claims of psychical researchers that, without bothering to examine the evidence, they rushed into condemnatory print in terms so strongly emotive that, in any other field of scientific research, they would have lost any reputation they enjoyed.

One must not tumble, however, into the

Left: Katie King, allegedly a spirit materialised by the medium Florence Cook (visible at the left of the picture), photographed at a sitting in the home of Sir William Crookes. In the foreground is Dr Gully, another investigator. Katie was sufficiently substantial to be able to accept gifts of jewellery from an admirer. Crookes was one of the most eminent of those scientists who were open-minded enough to investigate mediumship and courageous enough to vouch for its authenticity

Below: dark ectoplasm is extruded from the navel of 'Margery' (Mrs Mina Crandon), an American medium active during the 1920s. Margery sat for a committee that was appointed by the magazine *Scientific American*. Her failure to convince them helped to strengthen the widespread conviction that science was in conflict with psychical claims. She was proved guilty of fraud on another occasion

common pitfall of believing that because a pioneer is at odds with the establishment regarding alleged new discoveries, he or she must be progressive, an unacknowledged genius unjustly persecuted by a hidebound and reactionary authority. As Marx put it – Groucho, not Karl –

> They said Galileo was mad, and he was proved right. They laughed at the Wright brothers, but they *did* fly. They thought my uncle Waldorf was cuckoo – and he was as mad as a hatter!

There is, of course, another strong motive for immediate antagonism towards psychical research and its findings from the intellectual establishments – a motive best expressed as a sort of equation of irrational identification:

> psychical research = spiritualism = the occult = black magic = witchcraft = the superstitious dark ages from which science has rescued mankind

In the second half of the 19th century especially, scientists and other learned men looked back in horror at the follies, the cruelties and the miseries imposed on the population of Europe by the superstitious persecution of 'witches'. It is estimated that during the witchcraft mania a quarter of a million people suffered torture and a hideous death at the hands of their tormentors. Nineteenth-century thinkers, having seen the light of science dispel the darkness of those earlier ages, were determined to withstand any movement that threatened to extinguish that light.

The belief in the impossibility of psychic phenomena was largely created because of the success of 19th-century science. It explained a host of celestial phenomena by applying Newton's law of gravitation and his laws of motion. One of the outstanding scientific successes of the century was the prediction of the existence of the planet Neptune, on the basis of its gravitational effects, before it was discovered with telescopes. Science came to understand a wide variety of natural phenomena, integrating in a seemingly universal theory of the physical world a large number of formerly separate fields, such as heat, light, electricity and magnetism. Clerk Maxwell's beautiful equations of electromagnetism gave an almost complete understanding of the electromagnetic field, leading ultimately to radio. In technology, too, Man's increasing use of his scientific knowledge in building bridges, ships, factories and trains, demonstrated how firmly based his mastery of nature was. It was not surprising that the only fear of scientists towards the end of the 19th century was that there seemed few, if any, jungles of ignorance left to be explored. One scientist expressed the belief that most scientific effort would henceforth be devoted to measuring physical constants to more decimal places.

The billiard-ball Universe

In this climate of opinion, most informed people believed that space, time, mass, the atom, energy, and so on were clearly understood. A body was made up ultimately of hard, billiard-ball-like atoms. Each atom always had a well-defined position and velocity. One could describe its space co-ordinates – its position – to any desired degree of accuracy, and by bringing in Newtonian time, which flowed uniformly, the rate of change of its space co-ordinates – its speed – could be expressed uniquely. Matter was indestructible: it could change its form from solid to liquid to gas, but it could never disappear – or appear. Energy likewise was indestructible, though it, too, could change its form. The potential for useful work stored

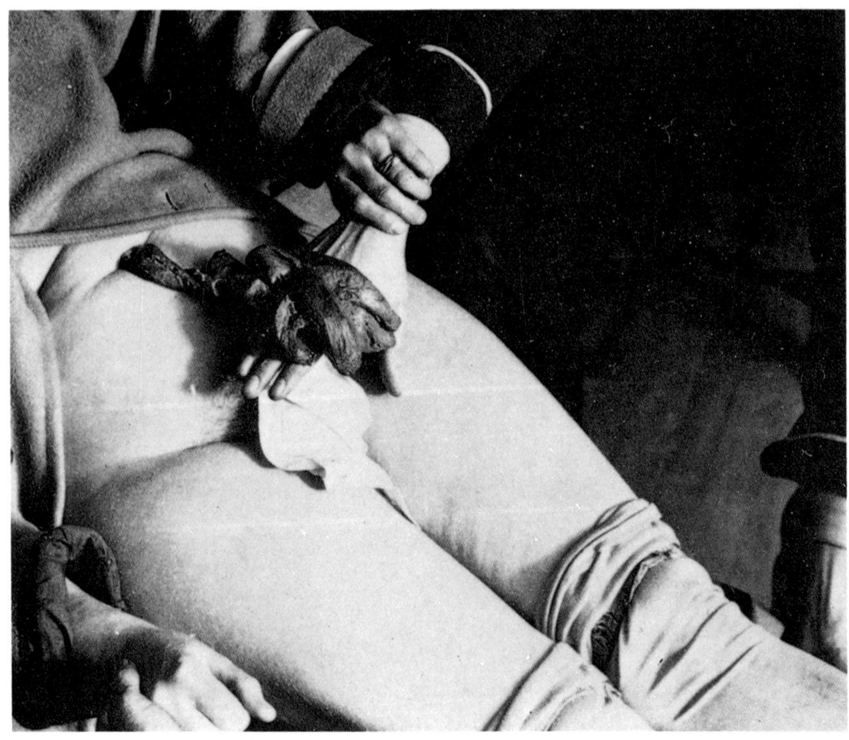

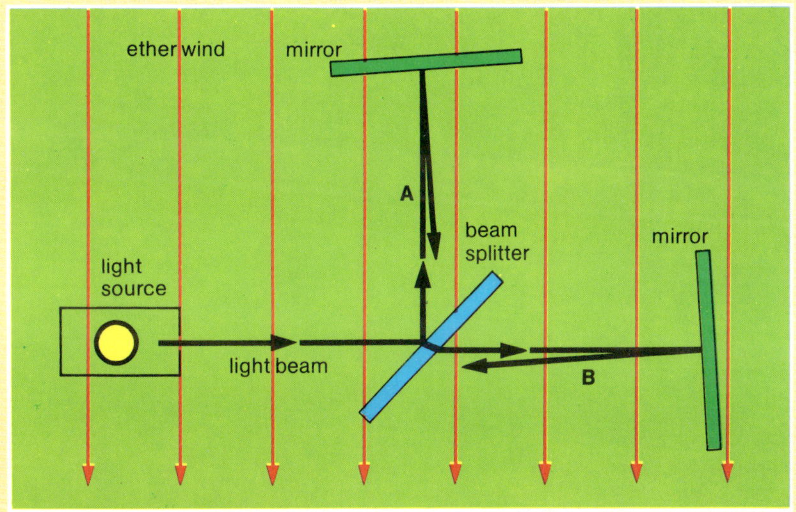

In search of the ether

Left: a massive table floating on mercury provided a stable support for the optical instruments used by Michelson and Morley

Below: a light ray is split into two components. One travels parallel to the supposed ether wind, one at right angles to it

The crisis of Victorian science was marked by many baffling experimental results. One of the most important was obtained by the American physicists A. A. Michelson and E. W. Morley in 1887. Light was a form of wave motion and so, it seemed, must be carried in some extraordinarily tenuous and all-pervasive fluid, as sound waves are carried in air. Since the Earth moves in its orbit around the Sun at 18 miles (30 kilometres) per second, a strong ether 'wind' must be blowing over the planet. Michelson and Morley devised a sensitive experiment to detect it. A light ray was sent to a 'beam splitter', a mirror that partly reflected and partly transmitted the light. The whole apparatus could

be rotated. In the orientation shown, one beam (A) would first be slowed down as it travelled against the ether wind, and then speeded up as it travelled with it. The net result would be that it took longer to make the round trip than beam B, which travelled across the ether wind. Michelson and Morley compared beams A and B and could find no difference in their travel times. Yet it was unthinkable that the Earth did not move. The only tenable solution was Einstein's theory of relativity, which abandoned the concept of the ether and drastically revised our ideas of space and time. Light is now regarded as sometimes behaving like a wave motion – though not requiring any physical medium for its transmission – and sometimes behaving like a stream of particles.

in a coiled spring, in an electric storage battery or in a hot gas was energy in its different manifestations.

It looked, too, as if the functions of plants and animals could ultimately be resolved into physical and chemical processes. Man, too, was beginning to be understood. The great physiologists and neurologists such as Hughlings Jackson seemed to be demonstrating by their pioneer studies of neural processes that a sound mind presupposed a sound brain. The impairment of personality and mental functions caused by brain lesions of various kinds led many to the belief that the concept of 'mind' was superfluous. More and more researchers were adhering to 'epiphenomenalism', which asserted that mental events were purely a side effect of brain activity – reflecting it but not influencing it, so that an understanding of brain activity would be sufficient for an understanding of all mental processes.

There were two other major theories, though they were losing their adherents. Parallelism regarded mental and neural events as running in parallel, without either

The brilliant physicist James Clerk Maxwell, who conjectured that light waves were undulations in a subtle medium, the ether. The overthrow of the concept of the ether marked the fall of Victorian physics

being the cause of the other. This also made understanding of the brain sufficient for scientific purposes. Interactionism maintained that mind was as real as brain, existed separately from it, yet interacted with it. This would make an understanding of mental processes dependent on, but not entirely reducible to, processes in the brain. Very few thinkers at the end of the 19th century still believed this.

As far as the soul was concerned, it is fair to say that a good proportion of intelligent people refused to entertain such an outmoded and elusive concept. Lip service was still paid to the Church but, more and more, death was looked upon as the final annihilator of all human hopes. Most people, in fact, refused to think seriously about it at all until faced by the grim reality. Frederic Myers, the great pioneer of psychical research, was once in the company of a Victorian businessman whom he attempted to engage in conversation about Man's possible survival after death. The businessman was obviously uneasy and embarrassed. He refused to discuss the matter. Finally Myers

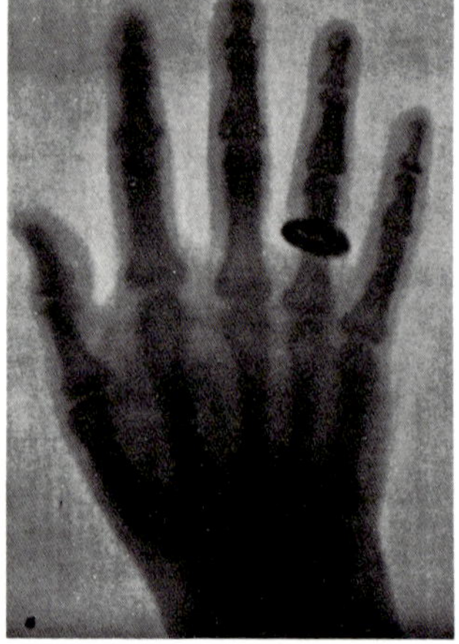

asked point blank: 'What do you think will happen to you when you die?' His companion's answer was: 'Why, I suppose I will enter into the joy of my Lord, but why talk about such an unpleasant subject?'

It is no wonder then that the alleged phenomena studied by psychical researchers found no lodging in the house of late-19th-century science. Telepathy, clairvoyance, psychokinesis, precognition and retro-cognition – all these branches of the para-normal were inexplicable according to the 19th-century world model. They were, in fact, downright impossible. Only a deluded and gullible fool would believe them.

And as if these weren't enough, what about the bizarre phenomena of the seance room, where mediums went into trances, were controlled by spirit guides and claimed to bring together the spirits of the dead and those still incarnate in this world? There were also many fully investigated cases of hauntings, both of places and of people.

Again, these things were impossible ac-cording to science and most scientists still ignored them or dismissed them with gener-alities about faulty reporting, fraud and human gullibility.

Yet among psychical researchers over the next century there were to be numbered some of the keenest and best-trained minds in Europe and the United States. For

Top: the Great Exhibition of 1851, held in London, showed off the machinery and manufactures of the Age of Progress. Superstition was in headlong retreat before science, which, it seemed, would make mankind the master of the planet

Above: matter proved to be transparent to x-rays – a 'paranormal' discovery of science, made by W. K. Röntgen in 1895

example, of the 52 presidents of the British Society for Psychical Research, 26 have held chairs in science or philosophy in uni-versities, 10 have been fellows of the Royal Society, four have held the Order of Merit and three have been Nobel laureates. They have included the physicists Lord Rayleigh, J. J. Thomson, and Sir Oliver Lodge, the philosophers Henri Bergson and Henry Sidgwick, the classical scholar Gilbert Murray, the psychologist and philosopher William James, and many others equally renowned for their intellect and research achievements.

A change of climate

The critical and condemnatory atmosphere of former times has to some extent changed since the 1950s. Controlled experiment in psychical research has confirmed the occur-rence of many types of psychic phenomena, such as telepathy, clairvoyance, psycho-metry, precognition and psychokinesis. For almost half a century, ever since the pio-neering researches of J. B. Rhine in the newly created Parapsychological Laboratory at Duke University in North Carolina, workers in various parts of the world have conducted carefully controlled laboratory experiments on the paranormal. They have amassed results that could not be due to mere chance. If these had been produced in some other, 'respectable', research field they would have been universally accepted as valid.

An increasingly large number of departments engaged in parapsychological research in the United States, Europe and Russia have enlisted the aid of modern science and technology. Among the more interesting have been the psychic dream experiments carried out at the Maimonides Medical Center in New York City, where dreams were analysed to see if they had been influenced by the pictures studied by experimenters in other rooms as the subjects slept. Similarly, at Cambridge University's Department of Psychology, Dr Carl Sargent and his collaborators found that scenes watched by others influenced the images in the minds of conscious volunteers who had been relaxed and subjected to sensory deprivation.

The new climate of opinion among professional scientists is mainly due to a growing realisation that the 19th-century model of the Universe is no longer valid. The physicists of the 20th century have demolished the old structure and in its place have installed a model possessing such wild properties that it makes the world of paranormal phenomena appear staid. With the construction of a new scientific world view, it no longer seems impossible that paranormal phenomena could be reconciled with science.

This new model could not have been foreseen by the Victorian physicist. It resulted from totally unexpected discoveries made towards the end of the 19th century. In

Warfare in the modern age – Vietnamese children flee a napalm strike on their village. In the 20th century human beings have inflicted suffering on each other on a larger scale than ever before. The human race – sadder and, perhaps, wiser than the crowds who thronged the Great Exhibition in 1851 – looks towards the future not with confidence but with a grim foreboding

1881 two American physicists, Michelson and Morley, tried to measure the Earth's velocity through the luminiferous ether, a medium supposed to carry light waves and to pervade the whole of space. They found themselves totally unable to detect its presence. It required the advent of Einstein's relativity theory to explain this baffling state of affairs.

In 1895 W. K. Röntgen discovered x-rays: a year later A. H. Becquerel noticed the blackening of an unexposed photographic plate in the presence of uranium and potassium compounds, thereby stumbling on

radioactivity. By 1897 J. J. Thomson had reached a stage in his epoch-making researches where he was able to show that electrons – electrically charged particles – were over 1000 times lighter than the lightest atoms. The first steps into the strange world of the atom had been taken. Soon Einstein published his first papers. At the same time late-Victorian certainty was being further shaken by a parallel revolution, stemming from the discovery of the subconscious mind. Freud and Jung were embarking on their researches, which were to demonstrate that Man was not even master of his inner sanctum, the mind. In the world of the psyche, laws operated that were as alien to common sense as the new laws of quantum mechanics.

The bestiality and irrationality still present in that psyche became all too plain during the 20th century. Science was the handmaiden of many of the century's worst excesses, and forfeited its claim to be the guardian of progress. Science was no longer regarded as possessing a veto over claims formerly considered superstitious – at the very time that its own internal development was permitting it to become more open to paranormal phenomena.

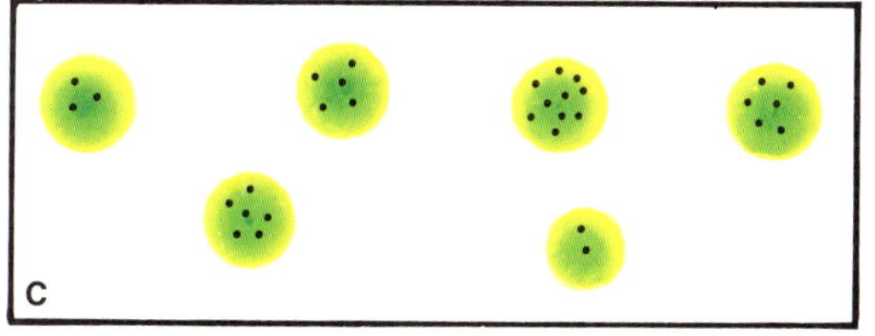

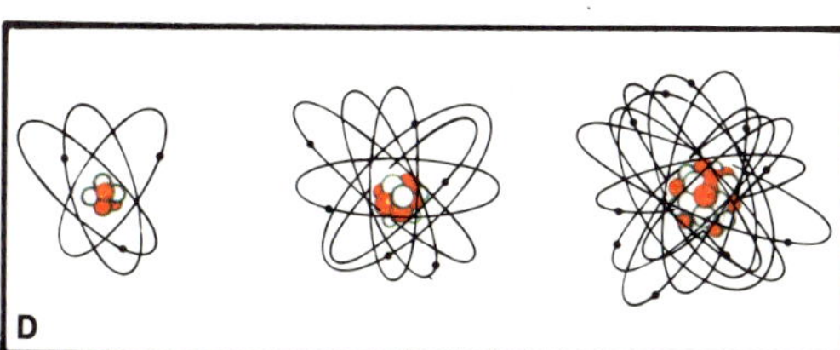

Left: the evolving concept of the atom. Democritus, a Greek thinker of 400 BC, regarded atoms as indivisible and made of one basic kind of 'stuff' (A). Differences in their shapes determined how they joined together and accounted for the properties of compounds. In 1803 John Dalton proposed that there were scores of qualitatively different types of atom (B). He was able to work out the relative weights of some of them. Only with the discovery of the electron was it realised that the atom was made up of smaller parts. J. J. Thomson suggested that atoms consist of electrons (negatively charged), surrounded by a cloud of positive charge (C). But Rutherford showed that electrons orbit around a central nucleus (D). Thus matter, apparently so solid, is largely empty space

During the 20th century, we have seen our theories about many basic concepts completely turned on their heads. In this chapter, we examine the incredible world of modern physics, where time flows at varying rates or even goes backwards, and where matter and antimatter are in constant flux

THE LATE-VICTORIAN MODEL of the Universe seemed a steady, reliable and enduring construction. Yet within half a century it was shattered by quantum mechanics and the theory of relativity.

The first suspicions that nature was not as it had seemed came when the Michelson-Morley experiment failed in its attempt to detect the movement of the Earth through the luminiferous ether (see page 21). The physicists Hendrik Lorentz and G. F. Fitzgerald suggested an explanation: physical objects had sizes that depended on their speeds – a moving object shrank in the direction of its motion. They also postulated that the measurement of the passage of time by a clock depended likewise on the clock's velocity. The expression 'time flies' took on quite a different meaning! They suggested that the Michelson-Morley null result could be explained by such changes in the measuring apparatus.

Lorentz gave a special mathematical expression that related the space and time

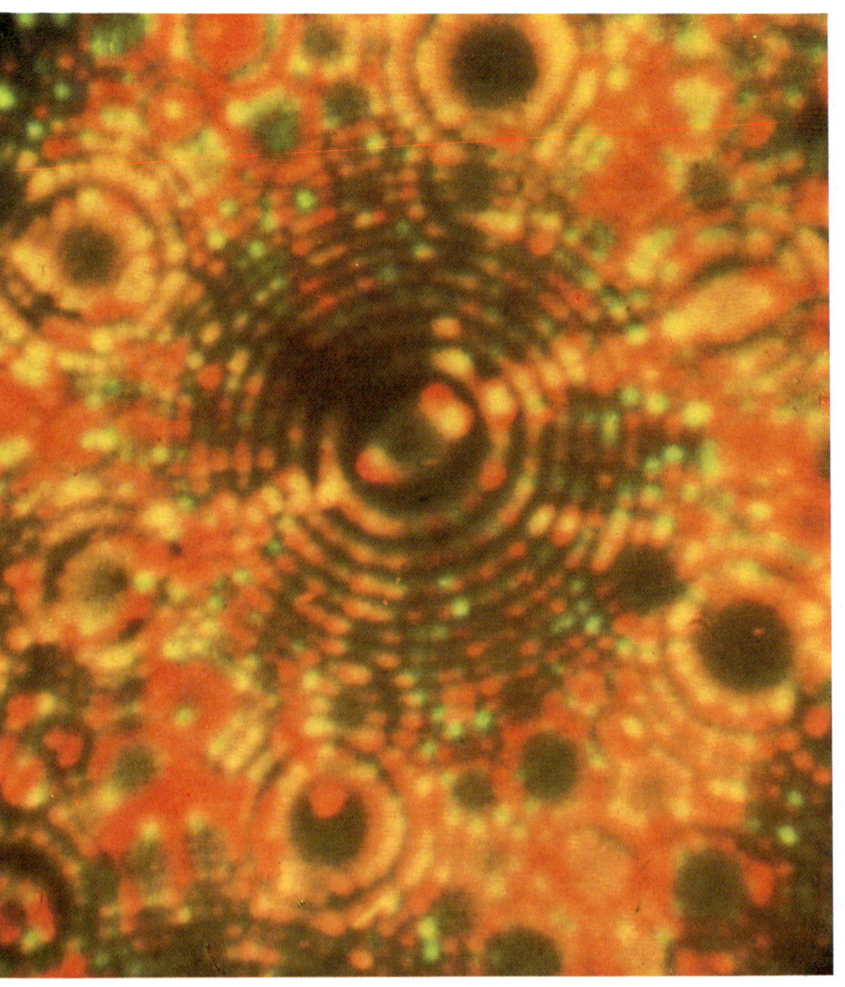

The phantom universe

measurements made by a moving observer to those made by an observer at rest. Speeds in Man's everyday life are very small with respect to the velocity of light – which is 186,000 miles per second (300,000 kilometres per second) – and so these effects would be unnoticeable. But if light travelled at the speed of, say, a racing car, then even in past centuries people might have taken it as quite normal for arrows and cannonballs to shorten perceptibly in the direction of travel, regaining their former length when they stopped, and for a clock's hands to turn more slowly while it was moving.

Some of Lorentz's ideas appeared, in a different form, in Einstein's theory of relativity, published in 1905. But Einstein went further by denying any distinction between moving and stationary objects. An observer in a high-speed rocket would see an apparent shortening of 'stationary' objects and a slowing down of 'stationary' clocks, just as observers on Earth would see these changes in him and in the rocket.

Einstein showed that this curious velocity effect also altered the mass of an object. As its velocity increased, its mass increased,

A photograph of individual atoms. Each spot of light in this picture represents a single atom in the tip of a tungsten needle. The symmetrical patterning of the atoms reflects the crystalline structure of the metal. To make the picture, an intense electric field was applied at the highly sharpened tip of the needle. Electrons were torn from each atom and formed images where they struck the film

making the object harder to accelerate. As its speed approached the velocity of light, the mass became enormous. Einstein obtained the result that the velocity of light was a limit that no physical object could reach. Nowadays, physicists are able to accelerate charged particles to within a few per cent of this velocity, at which speeds their masses are observed to be many times their rest mass.

In addition, Einstein assumed that the velocity of light as measured by any observer was a fixed quantity, no matter at what speed the observer moved. This again was contrary to common sense. If two cars, each travelling at 50 miles per hour (80 km/h) as measured by a stationary observer, are approaching each other, we would expect that an observer in one of the cars would see the other as approaching at 100 miles per hour (160 km/h). In fact, as Einstein showed, the relative speed is actually less than this by an infinitesimal amount (see page 42).

Furthermore, if the cars were beams of light, and the speed of light were only 50 miles per hour (80 km/h), then a measurement of its speed would always give that result – no matter what the speed of the observer. In essence, he would be carrying out Michelson and Morley's experiment, and finding what they found – that no variation in the speed of light is detectable.

Treating space and time as separate and independent quantities was now shown to be mistaken. In 1908 Hermann Minkowski suggested that the concept of 'spacetime' could be used to remove the barriers to our acceptance of such strange effects as these changes in time and size. He claimed:

> Henceforth space by itself, and time by itself, are doomed to fade away into mere shadows, and only a kind of union of the two will preserve an independent reality.

In Minkowski's conception the Universe is represented as having four dimensions: the three dimensions of space – length, breadth and width – and the dimension of time. The history of a body (a human being, a picture, anything) is represented by a 'world line', mapping its course through space and time from its creation to its dissolution. There is no movement or change in this representation of the Universe. Past, present and future are introduced by human consciousness. The slice of space-time consciously perceived defines the present moment for the observer. Some theorists have supposed that consciousness travels like a tiny point of light along the observer's world line. Although the four-dimensional block Universe is static and unchanging, he is under the illusion that 'things happen' – rather like the illusion experienced by a driver at night when trees that are actually static seem to appear in the headlamp's beam, rush past and disappear.

On closer examination this model of space, time and consciousness reveals difficulties, but it remains useful when paranormal phenomena relating to time and consciousness are studied, if only to help the theorist break free from common-sense conceptions or prejudices about such matters.

Into the atom

After the theories of Einstein and Minkowski, still worse assaults on common sense were to follow. J. J. Thomson showed that the electron was an entity with less than a thousandth of the mass of the hydrogen atom. Other experimenters discovered the proton and the neutron. Both had essentially the same mass as a hydrogen atom but, whereas the proton carried a charge equal to that of the electron but of opposite sign, the neutron was electrically neutral. Ernest Rutherford postulated that every atom consisted of a nucleus of protons and neutrons surrounded by a screen of electrons, held in orbit by the attractive force between their negative electrical charges and the protons' positive charges. The electrons circled the nucleus like miniature planets moving round a miniature Sun. Like our solar system, the atom now became largely composed of nothing. If it had been a sphere the size of the

Above: Hermann Minkowski, who conceived 'space-time'

Below: a snooker game, shown in 'snapshots' (left), from the bottom upwards, and in space-time (right), in which the vertical dimension represents time. Each object's history is shown by its 'world line'

Earth, then the nucleus would be a cathedral at its centre, circled by electrons the size of bungalows.

But the Danish theorist Niels Bohr went further. To any orbital radius there corresponded an energy level. Using the long-established idea that in atomic processes energy comes in multiples of a basic energy unit, the 'quantum', he showed that only certain orbits were possible for the electrons in atoms. But the theory gave little insight as to why such limitations should exist in nature. Furthermore, electrons apparently jumped from one orbit to another instantaneously. But even though the theory's assumptions seemed against all common sense, it became accepted because it worked.

Other researchers were now demonstrating additional strange features of these sub-atomic particles. When an electron collided with another atomic particle, it behaved like a tiny cannonball, but in other experiments electrons behaved as if they were made up of waves, as light is. The electron could equally well be regarded as a wave or as a particle. Sir William Bragg quipped: 'Electrons seem to be waves on Mondays, Wednesdays and Fridays, and particles on Tuesdays, Thursdays and Saturdays.' Perhaps on Sundays they took the day off to recover from their Jekyll and Hyde transformations.

This dual quality of the particles of nature is recognised in Bohr's principle of complementarity:

The concept of complementarity is

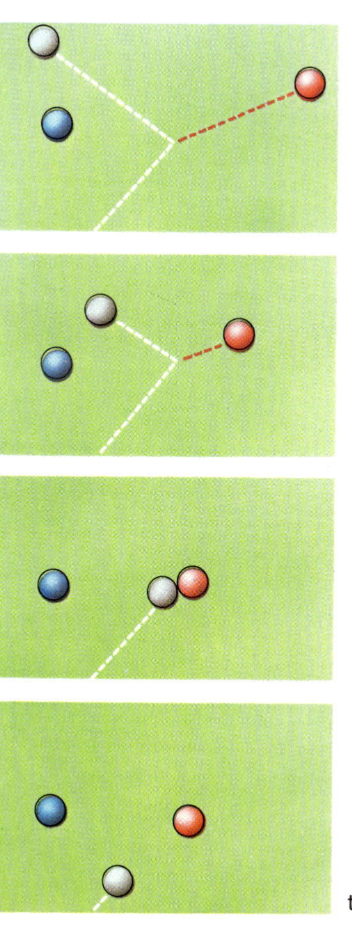

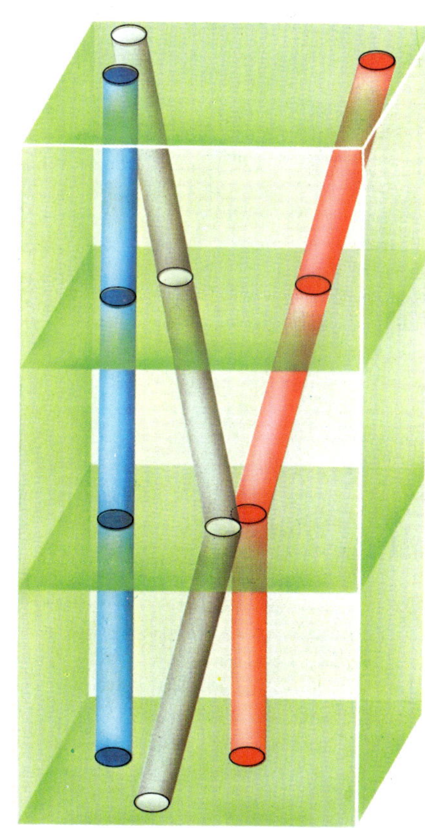

Left: the atom, once thought to be indivisible, has a complex structure. Swarms of electrons, carrying negative electric charge, circle a heavy nucleus consisting of positively charged protons and uncharged neutrons. The electrons follow orbits grouped in 'shells', and are responsible for the atom's chemical properties

Below: Niels Bohr proposed in 1913 that in the atom only certain orbits are 'allowed' for electrons – a restriction that could not then be explained

meant to describe a situation in which we can look at one and the same event through two different frames of reference. These two frames mutually exclude each other, and only the juxtaposition of these contradictory frames provides an exhaustive view of the appearances of the phenomena.

Bohr cited many examples of complementary relationships among ideas from outside physics: for example, moral *judgement* and psychological *explanation* of human actions may be mutually incompatible, yet equally necessary to give a full picture of them. Later we shall discover that the principle of complementarity can be usefully applied to the world of paranormal phenomena.

Werner Heisenberg, who had made crucial contributions to the task of replacing the 19th century's conception of a hard, material Universe by the insubstantial world-web of 20th-century theoretical physics, stated his principle of indeterminacy: that for subatomic entities it is impossible to know their position and velocity simultaneously and exactly. Since subatomic particles are wave-like it is not possible to talk about position in any precise fashion. In fact the equations of theoretical physics refer merely to possibilities or probabilities, not to facts. Henry Margenau said of them:

> The equations say nothing about masses moving; they regulate the behaviour of very abstract fields, certainly in many cases non-material fields. . . .

This field theory implies that matter is composed of wave-like processes, that the seemingly solid material Universe perceived by our physical senses is an illusion. In addition, the seeming separateness of objects within that Universe is also an illusion. On the subatomic scale, there are no 'objects' of invariant 'mass' and given 'volume' separated by 'distances' and acting on each other with 'forces' of the simple push-pull type of mechanics. The entity we conveniently call an electron has no definite position at a given time, no definite velocity and no isolation from the rest of the Universe. Quantum theory states that, whatever location is specified, there is a small but finite probability of

A crisis of identity

One of the triumphs of 19th-century science was the demonstration that light consists of waves. These were explained as consisting of fluctuations in electric and magnetic fields, and their wavelengths were accurately measured. But although the evidence for this view was overwhelming, it could not explain the fact that light waves can knock electrons out of atoms (below right). This 'photoelectric' effect is used in photographers' light meters – the electrons ejected by the light form an electric current, the strength of which indicates the intensity of the light. Even an extremely faint light can eject electrons – a fact baffling to physicists. Albert Einstein, in the same year that he proposed the theory of relativity, suggested that light behaves in this experiment as if consisting of a stream of particle-like 'photons'. This picture accounts for the behaviour of light in some experiments, while in others the wave picture must be used.

The same ambiguity was discovered in what had been regarded simply as

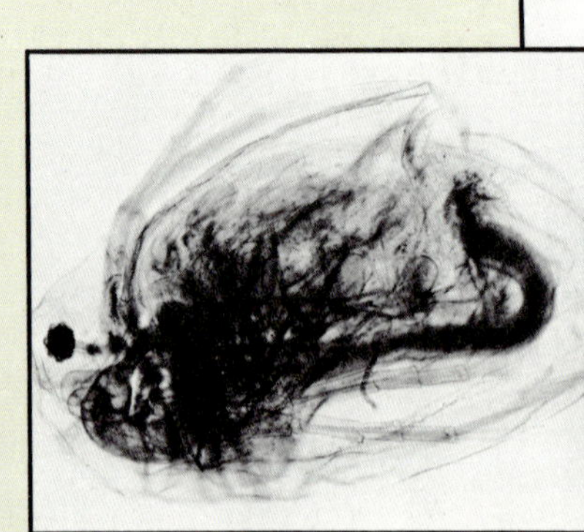

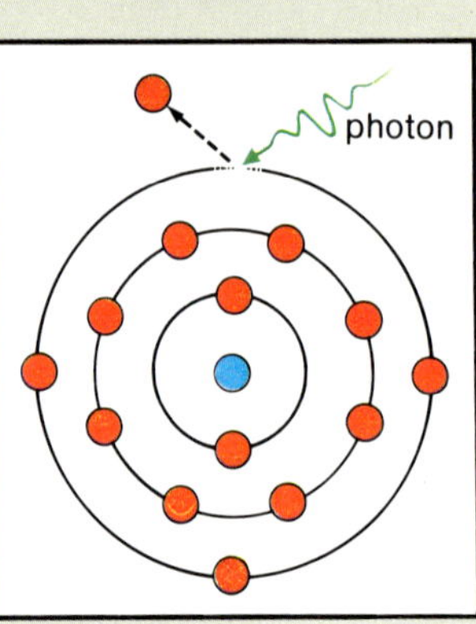

particles. The fact that electrons can sometimes behave like waves was demonstrated in 1926. Like the photoelectric effect, this phenomenon has practical uses. One type of electron microscope (above) uses a beam of electrons like a beam of light, focusing it and forming images of an object, such as that of the water flea (above left). The wavelength of the electrons is so short that they can reveal details hundreds of times smaller than those that can be seen with a light microscope.

the electron being there. It, and every other subatomic particle, is in some way related to every part of the Universe.

Instinctively we react to these ideas by assuming that the uncertainty in our knowledge of position, velocity, and so on is simply due to the imprecision of our measurements. But this is not so. The uncertainty is built into the microworld because of the nature of subatomic particles.

In countless experiments every day, mass is transformed into energy and vice versa; streams of neutrinos (particles that have no mass, no electric charge, no magnetic field), travelling from remote regions of space, pass through the 'solid' Earth, as if the planet were a ghost; experimenters work with 'antimatter' particles, the mirror opposites of the particles of the everyday Universe.

The existence of one such antimatter

A collision on the subatomic scale. The picture shows events in a bubble chamber, a tank filled with liquid hydrogen. A pion, a short-lived particle, enters at left. The hydrogen boils along its path, leaving a track of tiny bubbles. The pion strikes a hydrogen atom's nucleus, consisting of a single proton, which disintegrates to produce a cascade of particles. Their properties are revealed by the length, thickness and curvature of their paths

particle, the positron, was predicted by the British theorist P. A. M. Dirac in 1931 and confirmed experimentally in 1932 by Carl Anderson. It has the same mass as an electron but is of opposite electric charge. When it meets an electron, both are annihilated, resulting in the creation of high-energy gamma rays. The physicist Richard Feynman proposed that the positron *was* an electron – but an electron moving backwards in time. Certainly the mathematical theory suggested that if an electron could do this it would behave in experiments exactly like a

positron. Feynman went further, suggesting that all antimatter particles were ordinary particles travelling backwards in time.

Dirac had been led to his prediction from his study of the solutions of the quantum-mechanical equations that he himself had proposed. For every solution he found describing an electron of given energy, there was another one predicting an electron with negative energy of equal amount – no matter how large. But if these negative energy states existed, why did electrons not fall into these bottomless pits of negative energy, causing atoms to collapse and the Universe to be annihilated in one blaze of radiation? Dirac suggested that all the negative energy states were already occupied by an infinite 'sea' of electrons. Now Pauli's 'exclusion principle' states that two electrons cannot occupy the same energy niche; so, with all possible negative energy states filled, ordinary electrons are kept in existence.

Normally this infinite electron 'sea' is no more perceptible in atomic processes than the air around us is perceptible to our senses. On occasion, however, a negative-energy electron can acquire enough energy to climb out of its 'hole' in Dirac's sea. To the observer it then simply materialises as an ordinary electron. But the hole in the sea also becomes manifest, as an electron of positive electric charge – the anti-particle that Dirac had predicted, the positron.

Such paradoxical concepts have given Man the insight to manipulate the microworld, split the atom and, ultimately, create nuclear power stations. Emulating the legendary Prometheus, who stole fire from heaven, he now attempts in his fusion experiments to bring down to Earth the energy-releasing processes of the stars themselves. Some parapsychologists hope that our modern quantum-mechanical understanding of the Universe will inspire similarly fruitful theories in the equally strange field of the paranormal.

Below: P. A. M. Dirac suggested the existence of a 'sea' of unperceived electrons of negative energy (left). Ordinary electrons have positive energy. A photon of very high energy can knock an electron from the 'sea' (right). The electron appears to be created, together with a 'hole' in the sea – an anti-electron, or positron

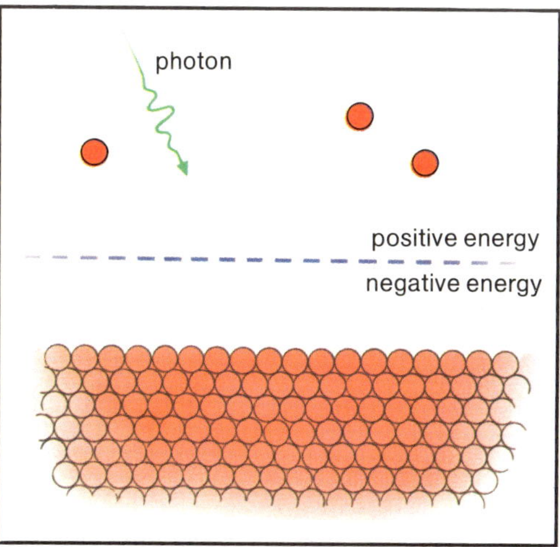

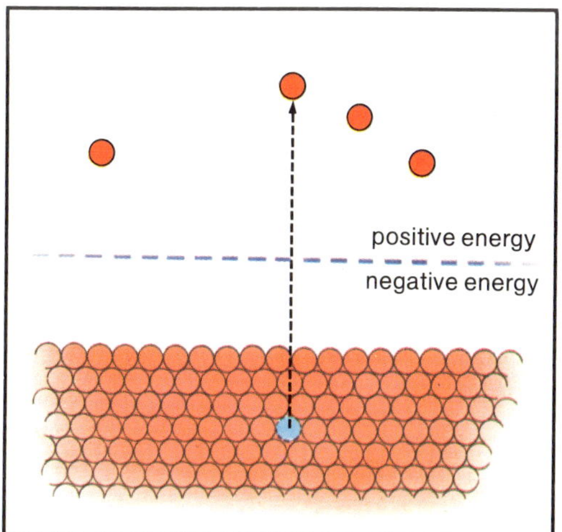

The new view of reality

The mind seems able to leap over barriers not only of time but also of space, and even death. Daring attempts have been made to account for these strange human powers in terms of modern science

THE STRANGE and beautiful Universe discovered by the brilliant researches of 20th-century physicists is forever hidden from our senses, adapted as they are to the macroworld. The entities of the subatomic Universe elude everyday concepts: they are related to each other in a web of mathematical probabilities in a shadow game whose rules are the laws of relativity and quantum physics. The statements of physicists about the nature of reality and about the immediate sensory world resemble more and more the statements of mystics, both eastern and western, and those of mediums regarding the operations of their psychic faculties.

The medium, the mystic and the physicist find themselves in unexpected accord. The odd man out is the one who still believes that the 19th-century picture of the Universe is adequate to the whole of reality. A few quotations are sufficient to illustrate this.

The physicist Sir Arthur Eddington: 'The stuff of the world is mind stuff.'

The mystic Evelyn Underhill: 'The game of give and take that goes on between the human consciousness and the external world. . . .'

The physicist Louis de Broglie: 'In space-time everything which for each of us constitutes the past, the present, and the future is given *en bloc*. . . .'

The medium Eileen Garrett: 'In the ultimate nature of the Universe there are no divisions in time and space.'

The Zen Master Dogen: 'It is believed by most that time passes; in actual fact, it stays where it is. This idea of passing may be called time, but it is an incorrect idea, for since one sees it only as passing, one cannot understand that it stays just where it is.'

From a Buddhist text: 'It was taught by the Buddha . . . that . . . the past, the future, physical space . . . and individuals are nothing but names, forms of thought, words of common usage, merely superficial realities.'

The physicist Henry Margenau: 'The central recognition of the theory of relativity is that geometry is a construct of the intellect. Only when this discovery is accepted can the mind feel free to tamper with the time-honoured notions of space and time.'

The principle of complementarity was forced on theoretical physicists because of the dual nature of subatomic particles: they

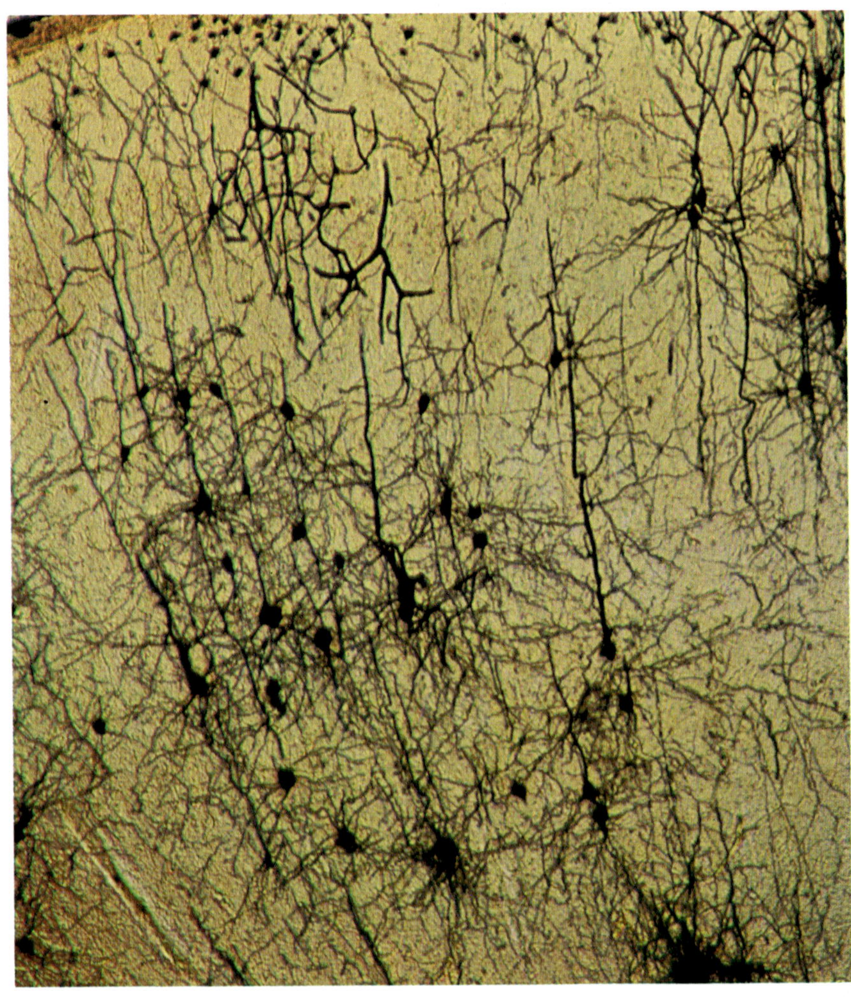

Below: Arthur Eddington, an innovative theorist, believed that the results of scientific research are largely determined by our methods of investigation – in studying nature we 'discover ourselves'

behave sometimes like traditional notions of particles, sometimes like waves. The principle is relevant in the paranormal field. The point of view provided by our senses in everyday life is evidently only one aspect of reality, a model geared towards a human being's immediate physical survival. The modern physicist's picture, totally different from the sensory one, represents nature in a different way, revealing quite different aspects of reality. Instead of conferring importance on objects, masses, positions, distances and a linear time of past, present and future, it emphasises patterns, fields and relationships in divisionless time. Individual identity is illusory, position a matter of probability. The physicist, from this second point of view, is able to set up experiments that reveal new aspects of nature and confirm his theories, or force him to modify them. The points of view of science and of common sense are complementary. Both work in their own fields.

Lawrence LeShan, medical man, psychologist and psychical researcher, has tabulated the characteristics of such viewpoints. His 'sensory reality' (SR) corresponds roughly to the sensory viewpoint: his 'clairvoyant reality' (CR) is the clairvoyant's or medium's view of the world. He finds that the CR view is not at all different in major respects from that of the modern theoretical physicist, or indeed from what the mystics of all ages have told us about the world.

One may then hope that psychic phenomena such as telepathy, clairvoyance, psychometry, precognition and retrocognition can take their place in a body of CR theory analogous to the theories of quantum mechanics and relativity. Like these theories, it may have to begin by agreeing that in the world of the paranormal ordinary concepts of space and time are inadmissible. There are

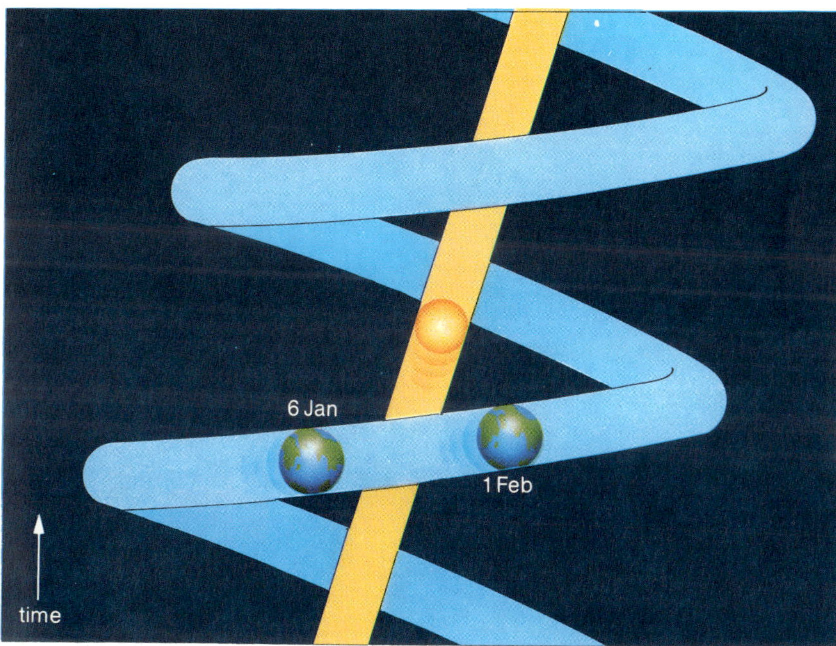

Left: some of the billions of cells in the outer layer of the brain. The extreme sensitivity of brain cells could explain how some people pick up 'psychic' impressions

Below: the physical distances involved in predictions are immense. An event on 1 February is not only 4 weeks later than one on 6 January – because of the movement of the Earth, it is also 42 million miles (67 million kilometres) away in space

indeed good grounds for believing this, since the ability of a sensitive to acquire information seems totally independent of distance or time intervals.

The sensitive and psychic detective Gerard Croiset could predict detailed events to be experienced during the following month by a person he had never met. In one case he made predictions on 6 January concerning the experiences of a woman, Mrs M, on 1 February. The idea of a brain-to-brain 'mental radio' breaks down here. What is not usually appreciated is that a further spatial difficulty arises if one supposes that Croiset's brain was somehow reading the physical memory traces that were to be laid down in Mrs M's brain a month later. On 1 February Mrs M was 42 million miles (67 million kilometres) away from Croiset's position on 6 January, because of the Earth's motion around the Sun. Thus it seems that mind cannot be localised in time and space.

What could correspond in the 'psychic mechanics' of clairvoyant reality to the non-material fields of quantum mechanics? Strangely enough, the first steps along the

Below: Lawrence LeShan, a medically trained parapsychologist in the United States, has made rigorous tests of the powers of psychics and mediums, notably the 'object-reading' abilities of Mrs Eileen Garrett

road to such a concept may have been taken by certain researchers in the very period when the demolition of 19th-century science was under way. At that time brilliant psychologists such as the American William James, the Austrian Sigmund Freud and the Swiss Carl Gustav Jung were exploring another world invisible to the senses: the world of the unconscious mind, the strange, often paradoxical operations of which covertly influenced human thoughts and actions. All three were interested in the paranormal – James and Jung intensely so – for the light it might shed on the dark continent of the psyche. James, the founding father of American psychology, used the idea of the 'block universe' (see page 27) in his attempts to understand the psychic phenomena. He postulated the concept of the 'specious present', a tiny interval of time containing everything being experienced by the individual at that moment. Jung, who later collaborated with the physicist Wolfgang Pauli in an attempt to come to grips with synchronicities (meaningful coincidences), was aware of the revolution in physics going on throughout his long life. He introduced the concept of the collective unconscious, in some ways related to James's own idea of a psychic repository or record of all human experience. A major feature of the Jungian collective unconscious, however, was that it was not merely a passive record but a dynamic, creative one, giving rise to dream, myth, religion and artistic creation.

The memory of the race

The existence of the collective unconscious – the racial memory of mankind – is supported by dream analysis, by the universality of myths and by paranormal phenomena. It looks, too, as if this great, submerged continent of the psyche exists outside space and time. Like an island in the ocean, each human mind lies separated from all others above the threshold of consciousness. But just as all islands join below the ocean surface, so Jungian teaching suggests that below the conscious level, at greater and greater depths of the psyche, there is a merging of each personal subconscious. As Jung himself put it:

> The deepest we can reach in our exploration of the unconscious mind is the layer where man is no longer a distinct individual, but where his mind widens out and merges into the mind of mankind – not the conscious mind, but the unconscious mind of mankind, where we are all the same.

The pioneers of quantum mechanics replaced gross matter with non-material fields, accepting that their nature was indefinable and only the laws of their behaviour could be sought. Similarly, the depth psychologists for the most part ignore questions regarding the nature or 'whereabouts' of the collective unconscious, seeking merely to discover and understand its laws by studying its transactions with human beings. Just as the theoretical physicists have recognised various kinds of subatomic particles within the fields they study and have deduced their laws of interaction, it may be expected that the explorers of the psyche – psychologists, psychoanalysts, psychical researchers – will discover more about the structures of the collective unconscious.

For example, if the collective unconscious is a record or psychic store of all human experience, does it contain, like an electronic computer, the 'program' of everyone who has ever lived? Is it possible that sensitives who enter a psychic state gain the ability to activate and 'run' certain programs – the programs of people now dead?

Running such a program may not be at all analogous to running a cassette on a tape recorder. The tape is passive, non-reactive and fixed in content. By contrast, there are pocket computers that are 'intelligent' enough to give you a very good game of chess. And it is possible to program computers with medical programs that can 'converse' with a patient via a screen and a typewriter keyboard so fluently that the patient finds it difficult to believe that he is not dealing with a sympathetic doctor.

When Rosemary Brown receives dictation of music from Liszt, Chopin and Beethoven, or Luiz Gasparetto's hands are guided by Picasso or Toulouse-Lautrec to paint pictures, are these two sensitives merely interacting with programs stored in the collective unconscious – programs that contain information not only on the lives of these great men,

Above: Sir John Eccles shared the 1963 Nobel prize for medicine for his researches on nerve cells. His work led him to speculate on the interaction between mind and brain

but also their musical and artistic techniques, their memories, their personality traits and even their drives?

It seems reasonable to suppose, if we accept the hypothesis of a collective unconscious stocked with records of the lives and personalities of every human being, that the 'communicators' contacted by mediums will behave according to the beliefs and knowledge possessed by their originals. The ghostly figure may still act as if it believed itself damned for its sins. It may still try to invoke the aid of the living to solve the problems it left behind at the end of its earthly life.

It is also reasonable to suppose that the words, pictures, music and other productions of such a communicator will be strongly influenced by the mind through which they

Above: the prolific artist Pablo Picasso who died in 1973. His genius seems to have survived – appearing in the 'automatic' paintings of some psychics, notably those of Luiz Gasparetto

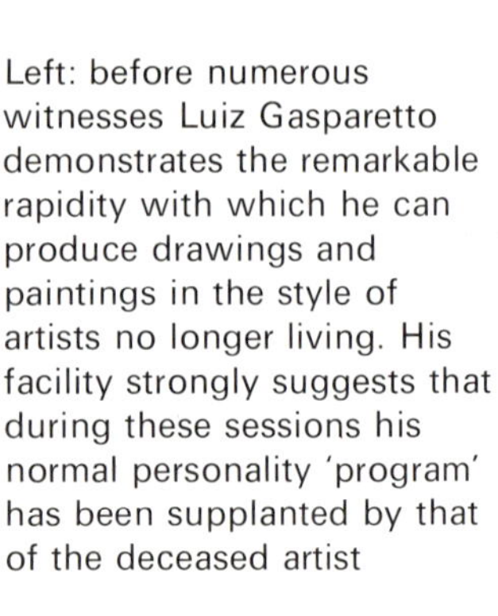

Left: before numerous witnesses Luiz Gasparetto demonstrates the remarkable rapidity with which he can produce drawings and paintings in the style of artists no longer living. His facility strongly suggests that during these sessions his normal personality 'program' has been supplanted by that of the deceased artist

are channelled – as the performance of a computer program is modified by the capabilities of the machine on which it is run.

This picture of human minds influencing and being influenced by the collective unconscious raises the mind-brain problem with increased force. The relationship between the mind and brain has long been a thorny problem for interactionists (see page 21). The mystery of how the will operates the brain and hence the neurones that control the muscles has been tackled by, among others, Sir John Eccles, the world-famous physiologist. Grossly over-simplifying his ingenious arguments, it may be said that the brain is a structure of an enormous number of neurones, many of which are critically poised between firing and not firing. Eccles suggests that tiny amounts of mental energy,

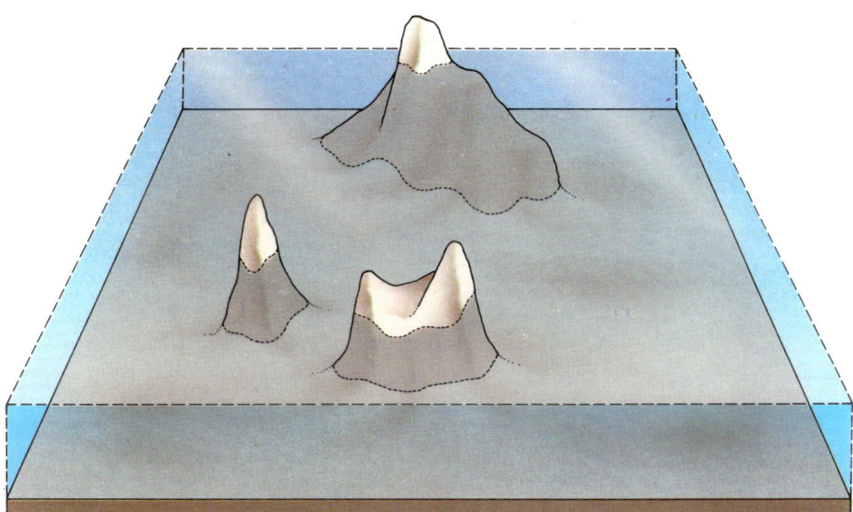

well-directed by the mind, will operate such 'hair-trigger' neurones by psychokinesis (PK). Each in its turn fires others, initiating in a fraction of a second a chain reaction involving hundreds of thousands of neurones. In this mind-brain influence, which would operate also in the other direction, we see the possibility of a theory incorporating some paranormal phenomena. If the minds of A and B connect at their deepest levels with the timeless collective unconscious (CU), sensory data entering A's brain could surface as imagery in B's brain.

Various researchers have attempted to generalise quantum mechanics to include paranormal phenomena. Martin Ruderfer suggested that neutrinos are responsible. Neutrinos are particles without electric charge and, to the best of our present knowledge, no mass. They react with matter extremely infrequently. In fact they are ghost-like in their behaviour: billions of neutrinos pass unimpeded through the Earth every second. Interstellar space is filled with neutrinos, created in nuclear reactions within the stars and travelling in all directions. This 'neutrino sea' might be capable of initiating psychic phenomena.

Adrian Dobbs, a mathematical physicist,

Top: a computer in combat with a chess master, David Levy (at keyboard). The computer could be given new skills by equipping it with a new program. In a similar way the mysterious abilities and knowledge that psychics can acquire may also be some kind of 'change of program'

Above: illustration of the interconnection of human minds, as conceived by Carl Jung. The conscious minds of individuals seem separated, as islands are separated by the ocean. Below the 'surface' each individual has a personal unconscious mind that is similarly isolated. But at the deepest level each mind merges with the collective unconscious, a shared racial memory that unites individuals as the ocean floor inks the world's islands

put forward a two-dimensional model of time and postulated the existence of 'psi-trons', particles that travel faster than light and can never be slowed below the speed of light. (This concept is in accordance with orthodox relativity theory.) In his closely argued theory (no more bizarre than much of quantum mechanics) he tries to account for telepathy and precognition.

The physicist and parapsychologist Helmut Schmidt persuaded volunteers to try to predict single quantum processes: emissions of electrons from a radioactive strontium 90 source. The time of occurrence of such an event is completely unpredictable and yet Schmidt's volunteers obtained scores that would have been expected to happen by chance only once in every thousand million experiments. It is, to understate it, difficult to explain Schmidt's experiments without invoking precognition or psychokinesis. If the former is involved, the mind is acquiring information about future events. If the latter, then the mind is causing events on the subatomic level, in a manner recalling Eddington's assertion, quoted at the beginning of this chapter, that the world is made of 'mind stuff'.

We are still at the beginning of our understanding of such matters. Some new Einstein or Newton may already be waiting in the wings to show how a more generalised quantum-mechanical model will embrace paranormal phenomena. On the other hand, it may be that quantum mechanics will be of value to the study of the paranormal only by the shining example of its creators' courage in postulating totally new and seemingly irrational concepts. On one famous occasion the sign of approval bestowed on a new scientific idea was the reaction: 'It's just mad enough to be right!' Perhaps a scientific theory of the paranormal will have to be very mad to stand a chance of being right.

Subatomic particles that are separated in space and time behave as if they 'know' about each other. Physicist David Bohm has attempted to account for this profound unity of the world – a unity that might explain some paranormal phenomena

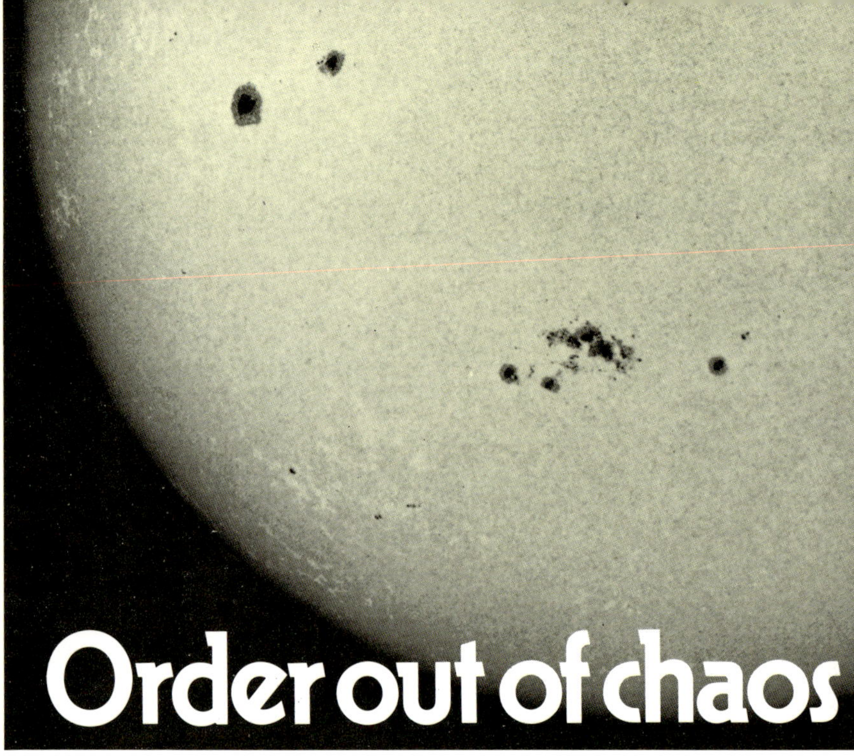

Order out of chaos

MOST OF US have had the experience of standing on a bridge, watching a rain-swollen river slip by beneath, its surface deceptively calm. Only the occasional eddy reveals the vicious undertow of unseen currents.

On the Sun's surface, 'eddies' immensely greater, often as large as the Earth itself, are often visible. These sunspots, regions of swirling gas thousands of degrees cooler than the rest of the Sun's surface, move with the Sun's rotation. They travel in pairs, the members of a pair being termed the 'leader' and the 'follower'. Study of their light shows that each spot has a magnetic field. And even though they may be thousands of miles apart, if the leader has north magnetic polarity, the follower invariably has south magnetic polarity, and vice versa. How does the follower 'know' the polarity of the leader so that it can 'decide' to be of opposite polarity?

This question is extremely easy to answer. If we could delve deep into the Sun – that is, add a third dimension to our appreciation of the problem – we would discover that each member of a sunspot pair is a 'broken end'

Below: the unseen bond between sunspots. A vortex forms beneath the Sun's surface, generating a magnetic field with jumbled lines of force. The field lines 'float' to the surface, dragging the vortex with them. Where they break through, two sunspots of opposite polarities form, bound together by the field

formed when a twisting, rope-like vortex of gas is forced upwards from the Sun's depths and 'snaps' at the surface. The two sunspots therefore rotate, in opposite directions. Since this rotation causes the magnetic field, the spots display opposite magnetic polarities.

The connection between the sunspots is easily explained. But quantum mechanics suggests a large-scale interconnection among particles in the Universe that is not so easy to understand. The problem is shown in an acute form in a famous paradox presented by Albert Einstein with two collaborators, Nathan Rosen and Boris Podolsky, in 1935. It states an inescapable conclusion of quantum mechanics that seems outrageously incompatible with the theory of relativity and the belief that the velocity of light is a maximum limiting velocity for everything.

Suppose an electron and its anti-particle, a positron (see page 26), collide with each other. They vanish and are converted into pure energy – two photons, which fly apart like shrapnel from an exploding grenade. In subsequent measurements the two photons are found to have opposite 'polarisations'. To understand polarisation, it is necessary to use the wave 'picture' of light.

Light is said to be polarised when its waves all lie in one plane: thus a light beam travelling horizontally could be polarised so that its vibrations were all vertical. Alternatively, it could be polarised so that its vibrations were all horizontal, or at any orientation between these. (Ordinarily, light is unpolarised: its vibrations can lie at any orientation around the beam.)

Each photon travelling away from the mutual annihilation of the electron and positron can have any polarisation at all – but the other photon is then certain to be polarised at right angles to it. So by measuring the polarisation of one, we can predict the

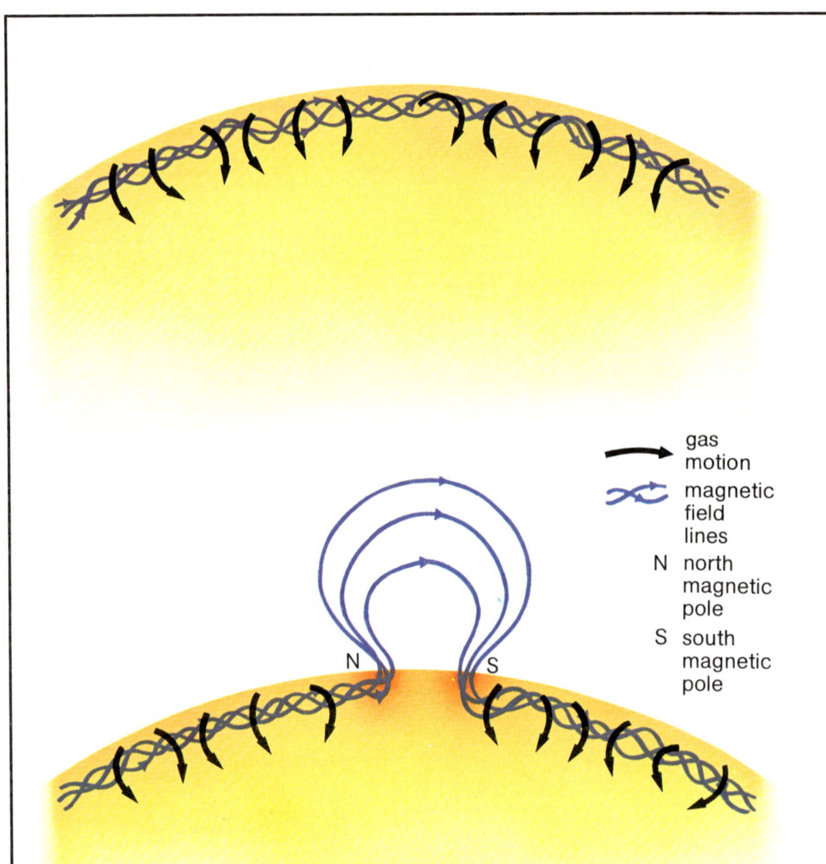

result of a measurement on the other.

The question asked by Einstein, Podolsky and Rosen can be put in these terms: why do polarisation measurements always produce corresponding results? Does some unknown influence – a 'signal' – travel from one to the other to produce agreement?

Such a question may seem as naïve as the question asked earlier about the magnetic polarities of the sunspot pair. Surely, it may be said, the polarisations of the two photons are fixed at the moment of the electron-positron annihilation, and remain the same thereafter. There is no need for a 'signal': the measuring instruments are merely discovering a pre-existing correlation.

But according to the standard interpretation of quantum mechanics, this is precisely what is *not* happening. The photons cannot be said to be in a definite state of polarisation before the measurement. The polarisation is 'potential' rather than actual: this is related to the fact that the results of

questioner supposed. These 'signals' would travel faster than light in some cases.

It is more likely that, as Niels Bohr argued in 1935, our common-sense way of viewing such experiments is at fault. Our tendency to split the experimental situation into independent quantities, such as the measuring instruments and the photons, and thinking of them as being localised in space and time, is a legacy from classical physics. Such a way of thinking is inadequate. Bohr went so far as to say: 'There are fundamental limitations met with in atomic physics, on the objective existence of phenomena independent of their means of observation.' This view seems to imply that the observer and his decisions play an integral part in actualising, or at least influencing, the Universe he observes; that in some deeper way the observer's measurements, the particles and the apparatus are all related and indivisible.

In *Wholeness and the implicate order*, published in 1980, David Bohm, professor of

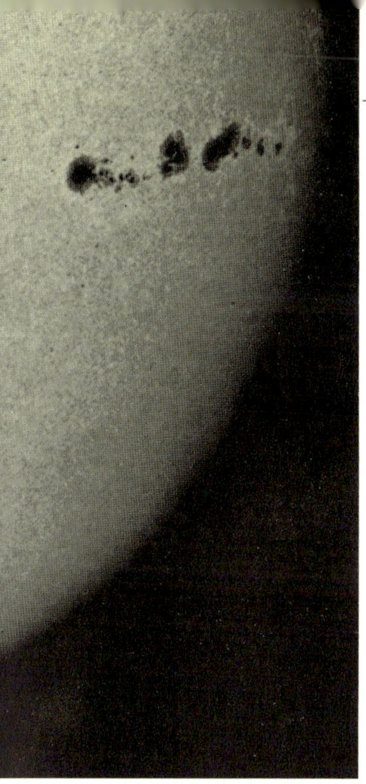

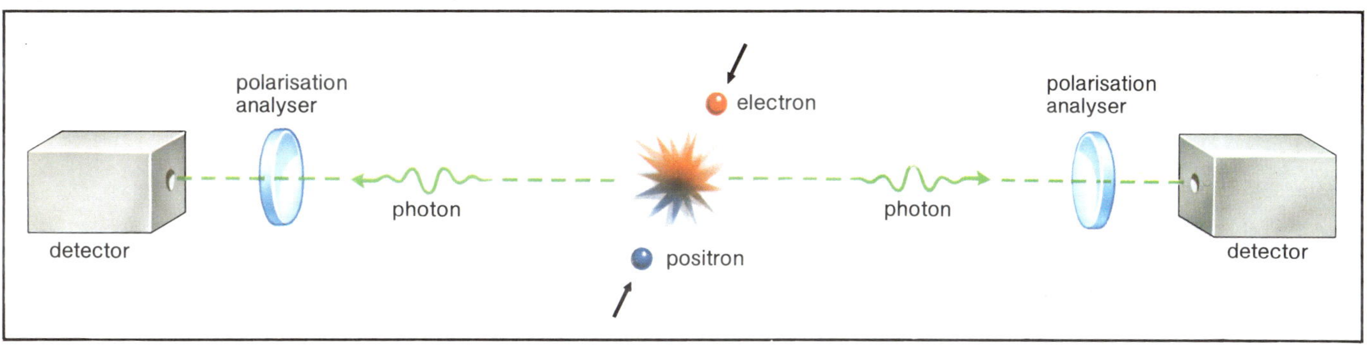

Top: sunspot groups big enough to engulf the Earth develop in linked pairs on the Sun's surface, and last for days or weeks before they disappear

Above: the paradox of Einstein, Podolsky and Rosen. An electron and its anti-particle, a positron, collide and are converted into two photons travelling apart. Each meets a polarisation analyser, which acts like Polaroid sunglasses: it blocks photons polarised at the 'wrong' angle. According to the usual interpretation, the photon now 'jumps' into a definite polarisation state, and is either passed or blocked by the analyser. The other photon, even though it may be extremely remote, also 'jumps' into a corresponding state, with a polarisation at right angles to that of the first. How does this correlation occur?

quantum-mechanical measurements are not fixed in advance – there is only a certain probability of a given result occurring.

Yet if each photon cannot be said to have a given state of polarisation before the measurement, how can the measurements at different places give correlated results?

An argument similar to this was used by Einstein and his collaborators as a weapon against the standard interpretation of quantum mechanics. They argued that quantum mechanics was fundamentally incomplete. Behind the properties physicists measure, such as polarisation, lie further, unknown properties, called 'hidden variables'. Variations in these 'hidden' properties would explain the variable results obtained in the polarisation measurements.

But Einstein's arguments were not accepted by the majority of physicists. And subsequent work by theorists has shown that, *if* the experimental results predicted by quantum mechanics are correct – and experiments are continuing to yield evidence of their correctness – and *if* hidden variables exist, then they behave very curiously indeed. In the electron-positron annihilation experiment, we could imagine a measurement on one of the photons sending some unknown kind of 'signal' that would influence the other photon – just as our 'naïve'

theoretical physics at Birkbeck College, London, describes a theory of quantum physics that treats such matters in an illuminatingly fresh, if controversial, way. The book is not easy to read, for it is dense with technical terms, often inadequately defined. But it should certainly be studied by anyone interested in theoretical physics and the nature of the connection between matter and consciousness.

Bohm argues that, although our separation of the world into a large number of seemingly autonomous objects has worked admirably in the development of our understanding and control of our environment, such a division is seen on a deeper level to be false. He puts forward reasons for believing that the level of reality manifesting itself, the level that we study, is produced by the creative, flowing processes of a subworld. Objects and patterns are briefly thrown up, like the forms fleetingly seen in clouds. They seem to have a certain stability, exist for longer and shorter durations, and can be described by laws based on observation. But because they are manifested, or projected, from a deeper, more fundamental world of dynamic processes, certain anomalies or paradoxes occur. They reveal that, however deeply we believe we have come to grips with ultimate reality, the artefacts we are studying are, as it were, projections into a lower number of dimensions from a higher-dimensional realm.

Bohm gives the rough analogy of a man watching two television sets, each showing the view transmitted from one of two cameras focused on a fish-tank. If the cameras focus through different walls of the tank, the two scenes watched by the man will be completely different. Nevertheless he will in time see a certain relationship between the images, a decided correlation of behaviour of the fish on one screen with that of the fish on the other. If he did not understand that the screens show two-dimensional aspects of an overriding three-dimensional reality, he might find the correlation puzzling and paradoxical. Bohm looks upon the Einstein-Podolsky-Rosen paradox and other aspects of quantum mechanics as hinting at this deeper, 'implicit' world.

He also points out that we should *expect*

An analogy for Bohm's 'implicate order'. We notice correlations among widely separated events (represented by the apparently unconnected television pictures) and deduce that they represent aspects of a single underlying reality, or implicate order (the three-dimensional scene in the studio). We cannot study the implicate order directly, just as the viewer knows nothing directly about the studio

problem to the sequence of steps by which he conveys his understanding to others.

The field of mental phenomena, however, is made explicit to us in a manner so different from that in which material entities are made manifest that we have traditionally held them to be completely separate, displaying such completely different natures that we have puzzled for millennia over such problems as how mind and matter could ever interact.

It is thought-provoking to apply Bohm's ideas concerning the transience of objects and the relationships among them to the world of human personality, of the conscious and unconscious minds. Does his theory make more comprehensible the interaction between individual minds and the deeper, more permanent world of the archetypes and the collective unconscious itself? Bohm is noncommittal, but believes that such problems, and the problems of the paranormal, are more likely to find a solution within the

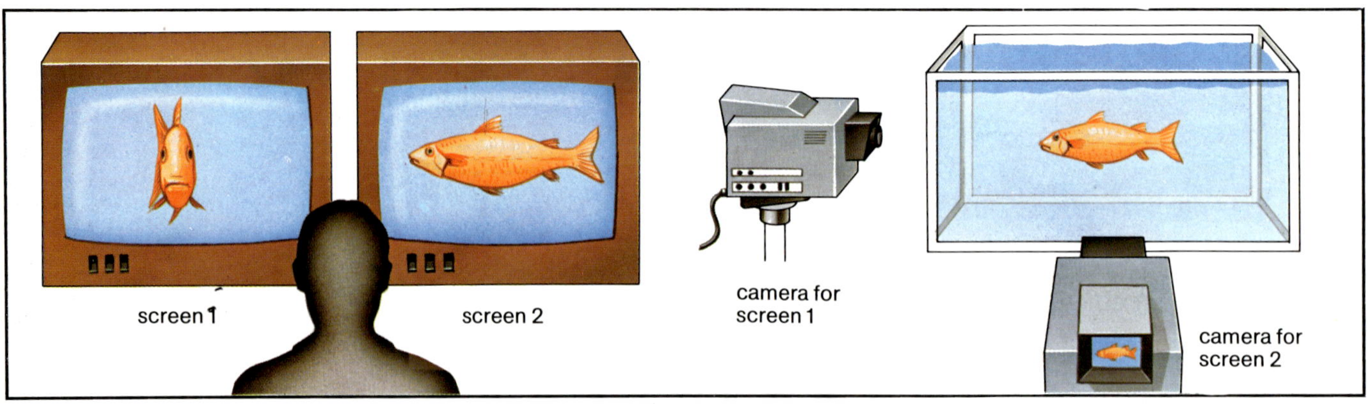

non-local, non-causal relationships between observed elements if these are projections of a higher-dimensional reality. One is reminded forcibly of the principle of acausal synchronicity formulated by Carl Jung and Wolfgang Pauli to describe the seemingly meaningful coincidences that occur in people's lives from time to time with such arresting force. By no stretch of the imagination can we see that their elements are connected by cause and effect and so, however striking an effect they produce on their observers, they are dismissed glibly as 'mere coincidences'. It may be that, like paradoxes, they should spur our minds to take fresh and original views of reality.

Bohm makes a courageous attempt to include mental events in his theory. The sequence of notes that we hear when listening to music is the 'explicit' aspect of the piece. When we understand the music sufficiently to grasp it 'in its wholeness', we are grasping its 'implicit' order. Mozart said that his compositions came to him as a whole, and he simply had to write them out. Bohm regards this as showing an intuitive grasp of an implicit order that could only be conveyed to others through the explicit ordering of the music. Similarly he contrasts a thinker's understanding of a logical or mathematical

framework of his ideas than they ever could in classical science.

Paranormal phenomena abound with paradoxes, those painful spurs to human thought. Telepathy and clairvoyance treat space with contempt. Precognitions seem to make nonsense of our most cherished conviction that cause always precedes effect, undermining our belief in time's orderliness. Such seeming paradoxes, like the Einstein-Podolsky-Rosen paradox, may be messages to us, drawing our attention to hidden realities. Careful study of the paranormal will guide us in uncovering, mapping and partially understanding such realms.

We have achieved the simple things, such as mastering flight, tapping and controlling atomic energy and sending members of our species to the Moon. In the paranormal we are facing the greatest challenge yet to our intellects. We should not expect to make fast progress, for we are entering areas yet more alien than quantum mechanics to everyday common-sense concepts. But we have plenty of time, if only we do not let our own stupidity wipe us from the face of our planet. In our uncertain world, the elusive phenomena of the paranormal are whispers of encouragement, glimpses of human personality beyond the physical and ephemeral.

The experience of two Englishwomen at Versailles in 1901 was to be a matter of controversy for years afterwards – for the ladies claimed to have walked back into the 18th century, to the time of Marie-Antoinette. JOAN FORMAN presents the complex case of the 'Trianon adventure'

ON A WARM AFTERNOON in August 1901 two middle-aged schoolteachers, Miss Anne Moberley and Miss Eleanor Jourdain, decided to enliven their Parisian holiday by visiting the Palace of Versailles, which neither of them had seen. Both women were interested in history, and both had some claim to academic standing, for Miss Moberley was the Principal of St Hugh's College, Oxford, while Miss Jourdain was head of a girls' school in Watford. Neither woman was inclined to be gullible or over-emotional in her reactions to her surroundings.

Having toured the Palace, they came to rest temporarily in the Galerie des Glaces. The open windows allowed the scent of the flowers in the gardens to tempt them out again in the direction of the Petit Trianon, the château built in the grounds of Versailles by Louis XV and given by his successor, Louis XVI, to Queen Marie-Antoinette. Eventually they came to a long lake with a woodland glade away to its right, and thence to another stretch of water, beside which rose the Grand Trianon, a château constructed for Louis XIV. This they passed on their left, before arriving at a broad, green drive.

They were not sure of their direction, and instead of walking down the drive, which led directly to the Petit Trianon, they crossed it and took a side lane. Miss Moberley noticed a woman shaking a white cloth out of the

When Miss Moberley and Miss Jourdain visited the Palace of Versailles on 10 August 1901, everything at first appeared to be perfectly normal. After leaving the Galeries des Glaces (right), they ventured out into the grounds to find the Petit Trianon (below), the small secluded mansion that had once belonged to Marie-Antoinette. It was then that they found themselves in what seemed to be another age.

window of a building at the corner of the lane and was surprised that her friend did not stop to ask the way. Miss Jourdain, she learned later, had not done so because she had seen neither woman nor building.

At this point the two ladies were unaware of anything odd in their surroundings and were absorbed in talk about England and friends there. They turned right, past some buildings, and glimpsed the end of a carved staircase through an open doorway; they did not pause but took the centre path of three that lay ahead of them, the only reason for

A stroll into the past

their choice being that two men appeared to be at work on it with a kind of wheelbarrow and a pointed spade. This suggested that they were gardeners, though the women thought their dress unusual – they were wearing long, greyish green coats and small, three-cornered hats. The two men directed them straight ahead, and the friends continued as before, still deep in conversation.

About this time both began to feel depressed (independently – they did not mention the fact to each other until later); they noticed a curious flatness about their surroundings, and each had the impression that the landscape had become two-dimensional. These sensations became overpowering as they approached 'a light garden kiosk, circular, and like a small bandstand, by which a man was sitting'. Neither lady liked the look of the man, for his face was dark and repulsive. He wore, they noticed, a cloak and sombrero-style hat. Although they were still unsure about which way to go, nothing would have induced them to pass the man at the kiosk.

The sound of running footsteps behind them came as a relief, yet when they turned the path was empty. However, Miss Moberley noticed another person standing nearby, who seemed to have appeared with some suddenness. He seemed to be 'distinctly a gentleman . . . tall, with large dark eyes and . . . crisp, curling black hair'. He, too, wore a sombrero and dark cloak, and he seemed excited as he directed them to the house. He smiled in what they regarded as a peculiar fashion, but when they had passed him and they turned round to call out their thanks, he had disappeared. They heard running footsteps again, which seemed close beside them, though they could see no one.

They crossed a bridge over a miniature ravine, noticing the small cascade that tumbled down beside it, and finally reached 'a square, solidly built, small country house'

Above: Miss Anne Moberley (left) and Miss Eleanor Jourdain (right). Determined to discover what lay behind their experience, the two women made further trips to the Petit Trianon, but found that the layout of the gardens had altered considerably since their first visit

with a terrace on the north and west sides. Miss Moberley saw, seated on the grass with her back to the terrace, a lady whom she thought to be busy sketching. The lady looked the women full in the face as they walked by. Miss Moberley commented that, though rather pretty, the lady's was not a young face, and she did not find herself attracted to its owner. This did not prevent her from noticing the lady's dress, which was of light material, with a low-cut fichu neckline; her plentiful fair hair was topped by a white, shady hat.

The two Englishwomen passed her without speaking and stepped up on to the terrace, Miss Moberley feeling as though she were walking in a dream. Then she caught sight of the lady again, this time from behind, and felt a wave of relief that Miss Jourdain had not paused to ask if they might enter the house. Miss Jourdain, as it happened, had not seen the figure at all.

They had now reached the south-west

Right: Marie-Antoinette (1775–1793), the Queen of France whose 'ghost' Miss Moberley believed she saw seated on the grass near the terrace of the Petit Trianon. It was the discovery that Miss Jourdain had not seen the figure at all that led the ladies to write down independent accounts of their expedition

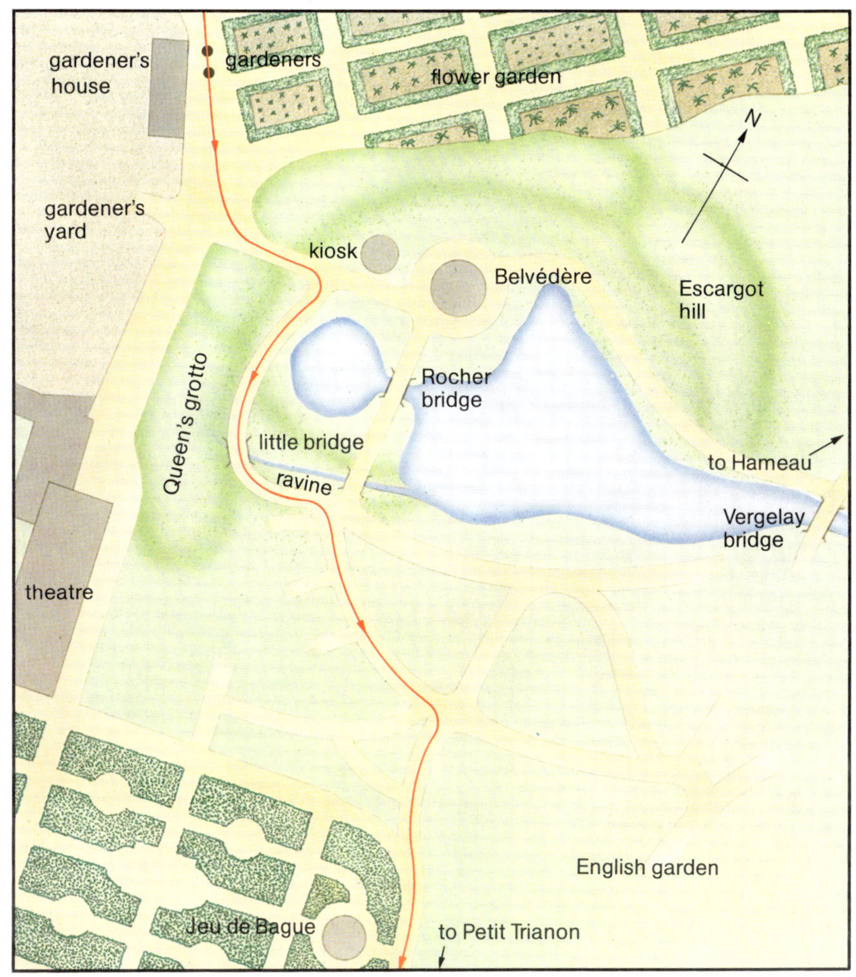

gardens of the Petit Trianon, wearing a pink dress and a floppy hat. The whole place – the people who were present and the amusements that were provided – had appeared, the friend said, to be an exact representation of Trianon on the fateful 10 August 1792, the day of the sacking of the Tuileries, the royal family's flight to Paris, the King's and Queen's imprisonment in the Temple. Miss Moberley and Miss Jourdain wondered if they had entered some memory of the Queen, either projected by her upon the Trianon or retained by the place itself. Mystified by what they had encountered, they determined to check the details of their experience with the facts by returning to Versailles.

A circle of influence

Miss Jourdain revisited Trianon alone the following January and again she sensed a hallucinatory quality about the place, born partly of atmosphere, partly of encounter. Certain aspects appeared different from those of the summer: the kiosk, for example, did not seem to be the same building, and at first there was no sense of eeriness. It was not until she walked over a bridge to reach the Hameau, where Queen Marie-Antoinette and her friends used to retire to play at being peasants, that she felt as though a line had been crossed, a circle of influence entered. She noticed a cart being filled with sticks by two labourers wearing tunics and hooded capes. She turned her head fractionally to look at the Hameau, and when she looked back, both men and cart had vanished.

There were other incidents – the sight of a cloaked man moving through trees, the rustle of silk dresses, a feeling of being hemmed in by throngs of invisible people, the sound of a distant band playing light music – but nothing to match the events of August 1901.

The two friends returned to Versailles several times afterwards but never relived their earlier experiences. On the contrary, they discovered that the plan of the garden

corner of the terrace. As they turned, they noticed a second house, from which emerged a young man (with 'the air of a footman'), who offered to show them the way round. They were presently joined by a lively wedding party, and their spirits revived.

During the following week the events of that afternoon were not discussed between them. It was not until Miss Moberley came to write her description of the events that she again experienced a sense of oppression, and she asked Miss Jourdain, 'Do you think the Petit Trianon is haunted?' Miss Jourdain did. It was only then that they compared notes and learned how their perceptions of certain events differed.

Full accounts were written by both women separately three months after their visit, and this lapse of time was one of the factors that gave rise to scepticism on the part of later commentators. Memories of an event recorded three months afterwards, they pointed out, were likely to be less accurate than those recorded within hours. In other words, the Misses Moberley and Jourdain were suspected of 'imaginative reconstruction' rather than accurate recollection.

Supportive legends relating to the Trianon existed, however. A Parisian friend of Miss Jourdain's told her that people from the village of Versailles had seen Marie-Antoinette one August day, seated in the

Below: a plan of the proposed gardens at the Petit Trianon, drawn in 1774 by the head gardener Antoine Richard. The ringed area shows a kiosk of the kind seen by Moberley and Jourdain, but there is no firm evidence that it was ever actually erected

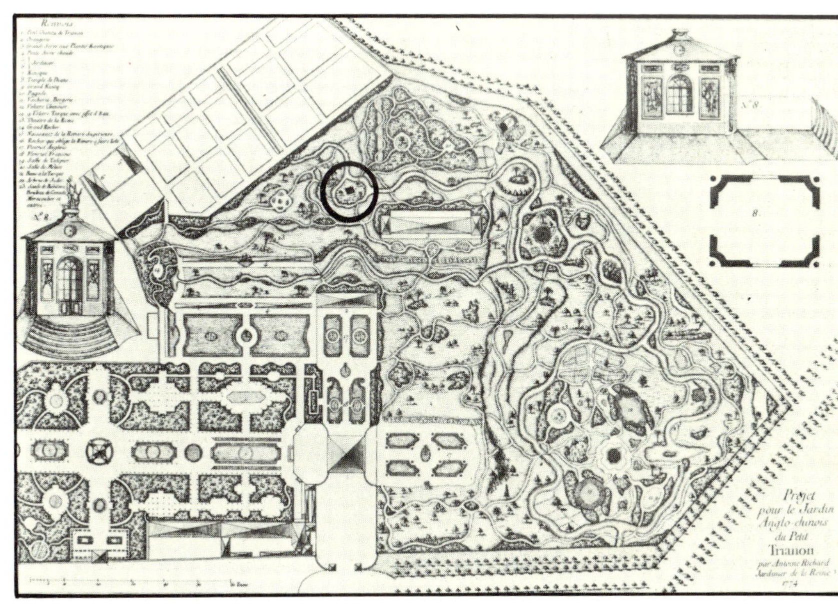

had changed considerably since their first visit. Woods had disappeared; paths had been removed; buildings had been altered; the kiosk had vanished; walls had been destroyed; the ravine, little bridge and cascade had all gone completely. The 20th-century Trianon bore little resemblance to the one they had originally seen. Mystified and intrigued, the two women undertook their own investigation into the history of Marie-Antoinette's Trianon.

It should be remembered that little was known about large-scale retrocognitive experiences at this date. Since the Moberley-Jourdain adventure was both intricate and complex, the simplest explanations seemed to be that the women had been hallucinating, that their memories had been inaccurate or that they were romanticising their experience; much was made too of the fact that neither woman realised *at the time* that she was seeing things that did not exist.

Miss Moberley and Miss Jourdain apparently felt sufficiently convinced of the strangeness of their experience to wish to check its facts, for over the next few years they took some trouble to research the details of the Trianon's original structure, of the way the gardens were landscaped and by whom, of the workmen who may have been employed there by the Queen, and of the uniforms that were thought to have been worn in her time. In the light of the results, the jibe of one reviewer that the women had seen *actual* 1901 people in *actual* 1901 settings and clothes does not appear to stand up to scrutiny. The gardeners' grey-green uniforms and tricorn hats were certainly not worn by officials at Trianon in 1901, for 'green was a Royal livery, and no one now wore it at Trianon', according to the records of Moberley and Jourdain's research, published in later editions of their book, *An*

During their research, Miss Moberley and Miss Jourdain found much evidence that confirmed their belief that they had slipped back into the world of Marie-Antoinette. Illustrations of costume of that period (left) showed a style of dress very similar to that worn by the people they had encountered. And, on reading descriptions of the Comte de Vaudreuil, a member of the Queen's close circle of friends (above), they concluded that he was the 'repulsive' man seated by the kiosk

Above: the Jeu de Bague, with its semicircular screen, which stood in the Trianon grounds. Léon Rey, one of the critics of the Moberley-Jourdain account, identified this as the kiosk, but the ladies disagreed

adventure. Could the apparitions have been masqueraders, the ghostly music that of a real orchestra playing out of sight? Perhaps, but why should masqueraders have been running through non-existent woods and along long-vanished paths on a hot August day in 1901? It may be objected that Moberley and Jourdain were themselves wandering through this very landscape at the time, but they were not running and were not in fancy dress. As for the music heard by Miss Jourdain in 1902, she discovered immediately afterwards that no band had been playing out of doors that afternoon.

Imaginative afterthought

The kiosk they had seen bore some resemblance to one that had figured in the original plans of Trianon as a *ruine* – that is, a decorative folly – but there is some doubt about whether it was ever built. In fact, the kiosk proved a source of difficulty, for Moberley and Jourdain, in their struggles to identify it with an original Trianon feature, tended to waver and to modify their opinions. It had 'a slightly Chinese effect', they thought. A French critic, Léon Rey, writing in the *Revue de Paris*, identified it with a building called the Jeu de Bague, which was vaguely Chinese in style. The two Englishwomen, however, disagreed with this and pointed out the discrepancies between the kiosk of 10 August 1901 – which, after all, they had seen and Rey had not – and the Jeu de Bague. Their reference to a 'Chinese effect' was not made until 1909, which does suggest imaginative afterthought; nevertheless, there are grounds for thinking that in 1774 Marie-Antoinette's head gardener, Antoine Richard, had sketched plans that included a light garden kiosk of the kind the two women thought they saw in 1901.

As one examines the 'facts' recounted by Moberley and Jourdain and the charges and counter-charges levelled against them over the years (well into the 1950s), their account and its interpretation grow increasingly confused. The swarthy man to whom the women felt such aversion was 'identified' as the Comte de Vaudreuil, who had played a sinister part in Marie-Antoinette's last few months as Queen, while yet another

critic suggested that the figure could have been that of the old Louis xv. There was hardly a point in the narrative of the two women that was not later challenged and often contradicted by some even wilder explanation for what they had seen than that originally put forward.

It would be tedious to retrace the steps of the Moberley-Jourdain researches over several years or to review the many ways in which the details of their adventure have been interpreted. Critics not only contradicted Moberley and Jourdain; they also contradicted each other, and leaned over backwards to show that the women had imagined what they had seen or had misinterpreted, distorted and romanticised it. Their researches had not been thoroughly or reliably carried out, said the critics; they had allowed later research to influence the evidence and had embroidered their experiences to accord with what they had discovered. The critics claimed, in other words, that Moberley and

Above: the Hameau, the miniature village built for Marie-Antoinette in the grounds of the Trianon. When Miss Jourdain went to Versailles alone in January 1902, she sensed nothing strange until she reached the village then, as she said later, 'the old oppressive feeling' of the previous year became particularly noticeable

Below: the Temple de l'Amour, which some critics believed could have been the kiosk, but which Moberley and Jourdain declared was definitely not the building they had seen in 1901

Jourdain had systematically cooked the books to produce proof of their story. The two ladies, whose intelligence seems to have been every bit the equal of that of their critics, were damned by implication as a couple of gullible elderly spinsters, whose heads were filled with romantic nonsense about the tragic Queen of France.

Yet this is not the impression gained from reading the Moberley-Jourdain papers. The women appear balanced, sensible and genuinely puzzled by what they encountered that August day in 1901. Their later enquiries are as thorough as opportunity and the availability of material could make them, and although the two women were accused of altering their original story to suit later-revealed facts, it may well be that they did not understand what they had seen until the discovery of certain facts made it clear to them. However, Moberley and Jourdain did fail to keep meticulous records and attested accounts of what had happened. It probably never occurred to them that these would be necessary to prove their veracity.

It is not possible to judge what actually happened on 10 August 1901. It seems likely that the women encountered a large-scale hallucination consistent with the conditions of a retrocognitive timeslip. And by far the most interesting aspect here is the sustained interchange that apparently took place between the figures from the past and those in the present.

Neither was the Versailles adventure unique in its scale, for two other English women underwent a similar experience at Dieppe some 50 years later. Is it the air of France or her history that promotes such curious encounters?

What were the disturbing noises heard by two Englishwomen at Puys in northern France in 1951? Were they, as the ladies themselves believed, the sounds of a 'replay' of the disastrous August raid on Dieppe in the Second World War?

THE TURN OF THE CENTURY saw two English ladies, Miss Jourdain and Miss Moberley, involved in an 'adventure' at the Petit Trianon, Versailles, in which they considered that they had a protracted hallucination of life at the château in its heyday. It was an unusual case, yet half a century later another pair of Englishwomen, Mrs Dorothy Norton and Miss Agnes Norton (both pseudonyms), experienced an hallucination similar in length if not in presentation.

They too were on holiday in France, at Puys, a village near Dieppe. Although they were sisters-in-law, they had not been on holiday together before. The two women

same length of time. The two women lay awake and listened to the extraordinary sounds that were reaching them, apparently from the beach. Dorothy afterwards described the noise as 'a roar that ebbed and flowed'. Finally, the pair turned on the light and went out on to the balcony, presumably to discover what was creating the disturbance; but although they looked down towards the beach, they were unable to see the shore or to detect the source of the noise.

There was no doubt that the sounds were coming from the direction of the beach, however, and they grew louder and louder. The women could distinguish different types of noise. Dorothy identified 'cries, guns and dive-bombing', with occasional shellfire; according to Agnes, the sounds were 'a mixture of gunfire, shellfire, dive-bombers, landing craft and men's cries'. Agnes also stated that 'all the sounds gave the impression of coming from a very long distance, i.e. like a broadcast from America, in unmistakable waves of sound.'

As they stood listening to the deafening

A sense of disaster

shared a bedroom on the second floor of a three-storey house that stood a short distance from the sea.

At 4.20 a.m. on 4 August 1951, Agnes got out of bed and felt her way across the room in the dark. As she reached the door, Dorothy asked her if she wished to turn on the light, but she did not. When Agnes returned a few minutes later, she asked, 'Can you hear that noise?' Dorothy could; in fact, she had been listening to it 'for about 20 minutes', according to the account she wrote later. Agnes said that she had heard the noise for about the

noise, the two women gradually came to the conclusion that the source of the sounds that were reaching them must be a paranormal one. Dorothy was no stranger to psychic experiences, for she had had several before, though only one of them had been purely auditory, as this one was. It had occurred five days before. Dorothy had been awakened by a similar noise, but she described it as fainter and less intense. 'At the end,' she said, 'I seemed to hear a lot of men singing.' The noise ended at cock-crow, and she then went back to sleep. Her sister-in-law, however,

had heard nothing and had not woken up.

However, critics who later disputed the women's claim that their experience was paranormal drew attention to one point. Dorothy and Agnes had had with them, throughout their vigil, a guide book that contained a brief account of the disastrous raid on Dieppe that had been made by British and Canadian forces on 19 August 1942. Both women admitted to investigators (G. W. Lambert and Kathleen Gay, whose report was published in the *Journal* of the Society for Psychical Research in May 1952) that they had known of the existence of the guide-book account, but they claimed that they had not read it before that night. Critics pointed out that the women had been in Puys just over a week when their experience occurred; it seemed remarkable that they should have shown so little curiosiy about the raid, which had taken place very close to where they were staying. Yet this appeared to be the case, for in a letter to the *Journal* of July 1952 Mr Lambert remarked, 'neither [Dorothy] nor [Agnes] was "interested" in the Dieppe raid, and had neither "read it up" nor had it brought forcibly to her attention shortly before the experience.'

Inevitably, though, the nature and sequence of Agnes's and Dorothy's experience suggested to them the Dieppe raid of 1942. As they stood on the balcony during the course of three hours, they both made detailed notes about the times at which they heard each type of sound. They compiled independent accounts the following day. There are small variations in the two records – for instance, the fact that while both agreed that the first burst of noise ceased at 4.50 a.m., Agnes claimed that a second burst began at 5.07, while her sister-in-law put the time at 5.05. Each had her own watch, but they admitted that Agnes's was generally the more reliable, as Dorothy's tended to lose slightly. (However, if the two watches showed the same time at 4.20, when the noise began, and at 4.50, when it ceased briefly, Dorothy's watch must have done more than lose 'slightly' to be two minutes slow at 5.07.) One fact may help to explain small discrepancies like this one. During the Second World War, Agnes had been a member of the Women's Royal Naval Service (WRNS). As a result of her training, she may have been more familiar than her sister-in-law with the techniques of accurate observation and recording.

The investigators, Lambert and Gay, drew up a detailed table contrasting what Agnes and Dorothy had heard, and when, with the timing of the wartime raid on Dieppe. The events of 19 August 1942 began

Scenes from the Allied raid on Dieppe, 19 August 1942, the sounds of which were allegedly heard by two English ladies nine years later. A combined land, sea and air operation, the attack was mounted as a preliminary to a full-scale invasion of German-occupied France – but it was a costly failure: of nearly 6100 British and Canadian troops, 3648 were killed, wounded, reported missing or captured

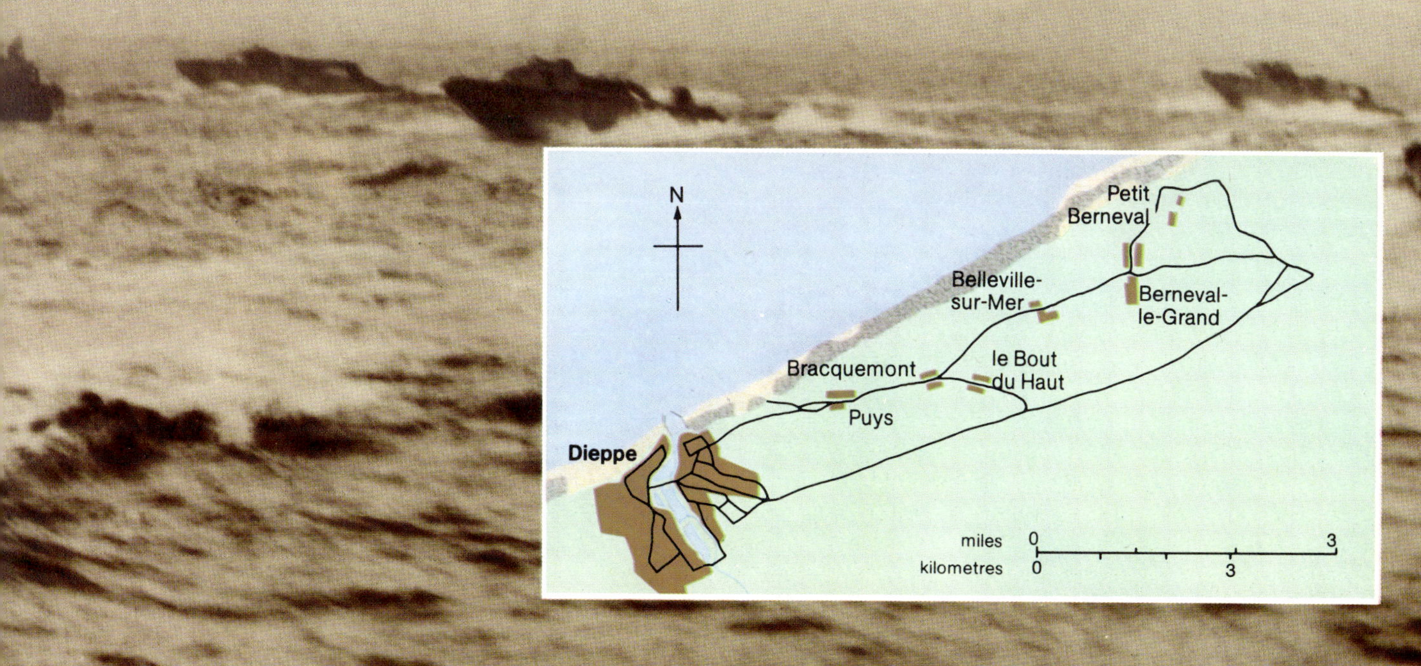

at 3.47 a.m., when assault vessels coming into Berneval ran into a German convoy. Firing began immediately, and the German defences at Puys appear to have been alerted, for when Allied landing craft ran ashore at Puys, they were met with heavy fire and suffered many casualties. Lambert and Gay suggested that the 'cries' heard by the two women may have been those of the German defence forces.

Zero hour for the tank landings at Puys and Berneval should have been 4.50 a.m., but they were delayed. The first wave of landing craft beached at Puys at 5.07, and by 5.12 destroyers had begun bombarding Dieppe. The main force started to land at Dieppe at 5.20. The seafront buildings were then already under attack from RAF Hurricanes, which had flown in at 5.15. At 5.40 the naval bombardment ceased altogether. Exactly 10 minutes later a further 48 RAF aircraft arrived and joined in the battle.

These chronological details were taken by Lambert and Gay from an account of the raid in *Norway, the Commandos, Dieppe* by Christopher Buckley. Neither of the women had seen this account at the time of their experience, and it is extremely unlikely that either knew of its existence. Furthermore, Agnes assured the investigators that even as a member of the WRNS, she had not had access to unpublished naval reports.

'An indescribable noise'

In general, the timing of the various sounds heard by Dorothy and Agnes coincided with the battle record. The points selected for comment by critics concerned the interpretation and identification of the sounds and the 'conditioning by expectation' of the two women, although one correspondent questioned the fact that although both Agnes and Dorothy had heard the noise before Agnes left the bedroom that night, neither woman had mentioned it. (This is not, perhaps, a very significant point, since Agnes had already reached the door before Dorothy revealed that she was awake too.) There was also some critical hair-splitting about the chronology of the women's accounts, but comments of this nature appeared less likely to upset the phenomenon theory than the information supplied by yet another correspondent, who proffered a natural explanation for the noises heard by the women.

In September 1968 Mr R. A. Eades reported to the Society for Psychical Research on a holiday he had spent with his family in France in late August 1951, during the course of which they had camped for one night to the east of Dieppe. That night they were awakened by 'an indescribable noise, which continued for several hours'. The Eades family discussed what they could hear and likened the noise to 'a zoo gone mad', 'a fair', 'an amplified, distant school playground'. However, they were convinced that it was none of these things, and in the town

Tanks and landing craft burning minutes after the battle. Dorothy and Agnes Norton claimed that the noises they heard in 1951 undoubtedly came from the direction of the beach, and that they could distinguish the sounds of gunfire, shellfire, dive-bombing, landing craft and men's cries

Guy W. Lambert who, together with Kathleen Gay, investigated the Dieppe raid case for the Society of Psychical Research

the following day they learned that a dredger had been at work in the harbour. The machine was still there, now lying idle.

Enquiries were then made of the harbour master of Dieppe by Mr G. W. Lambert, who wanted to ascertain whether or not the dredger had been operating during the night of 4 August 1951. The harbour master replied that it had been at work from 12.15 that night to 8.15 the next morning. However, dredging had begun some $3\frac{3}{4}$ hours before the battle noises started and had continued for approximately $1\frac{1}{4}$ hours after they stopped, which suggests that the noise of the dredger alone could not have accounted for Agnes's and Dorothy's insomnia.

Following a protracted correspondence in the SPR's *Journal* concerning the case, and the suggestion by Mr Eades that the whole matter should be reassessed by an independent investigation, an examination was conducted in 1969 by Mr Robert J. Hastings. He reviewed the evidence in detail and made the following points:

Although the two women had admitted a discrepancy of two minutes in the time shown by their respective watches, no attempt had apparently been made to check which watch, if either, kept accurate time.

Both Dorothy and Agnes had known about the wartime raid, but their information had been of a general, 'common-knowledge' kind and not detailed.

The women had admitted possessing a French guide book containing a description of the raid and had acknowledged that they read it on the balcony during their experience, some time between 5.07 and 5.40. They said that they had not read the account before then. They had made no attempt to conceal this information, but had offered it freely to the SPR investigators.

Hastings also commented on the coincidence of the Petit Trianon anniversary and

its possible influence on the women's experience. However, what seemed to him to be one of the most striking aspects of the Dieppe case was the fact that both women were aware *at the time* that their experience was probably paranormal. They were able to think that the sounds they heard were unusual, and to suspect that they might correspond to sounds that would have been heard during the raid. Such awareness is certainly most unusual and can only be compared with lucid dreams (which are also

relatively rare) in which the dreamer is conscious that he is dreaming. During a psychic experience, the conscious mind is generally taken unaware, and the subject is too busy coping with the extraordinary nature of the phenomenon to be able to consider the likelihood of its unreality.

Mr Hastings balked a bit at the fact that the women had omitted to mention activity in the air at the time of the 5.07 landing – particularly as he himself had discovered someone who had witnessed the air attack in 1942. Agnes and Dorothy had referred to aircraft, but Mr Hastings, acting as devil's advocate, suspected that the sounds were the normal ones of civil aircraft in 1951. On checking, he found out that Puys lay in the path of the regular London–Paris–Turin airway. Was that the sound the Norton ladies had heard?

The story of the Dieppe raid, as told by Dorothy and Agnes, contains certain inaccuracies. But so did the Moberley-Jourdain account of Versailles. Extended paranormal experiences rarely tally completely with the known facts. This may be because while a paranormal element is present – that is, information is being supplied by extrasensory sources – sensory sources are also feeding in 'normal' information. But the question remains: was either experience – that of Moberley and Jourdain or that of the Nortons – genuinely paranormal?

Two views of the Dieppe seafront, the main target of the Allied attack on 19 August 1942, at the time of the raid (above left), and at peace (below)

Analysing the French timeslips

Were events from the past really experienced by two pairs of English ladies on holiday in France 50 years apart? This chapter sums up the evidence for and against the alleged timeslips at Versailles and Dieppe

THE EXPERIENCES OF Miss Moberley and Miss Jourdain at Versailles in 1901 and of Mrs and Miss Norton at Puys, near Dieppe, in 1951 appear similar in some respects. Both experiences occured to two Englishwomen; the women in each case were on holiday together in France; the month in which both experiences occurred was August.

But here the parallels end. Moberley's and Jourdain's experience was both auditory and visual, whereas the Nortons' was wholly auditory. Furthermore, at Versailles the two women not only spoke to the people they saw but received replies from them (from the gentleman who directed them to the house, for instance, and from the footman who volunteered to show them the way). By contrast, Agnes and Dorothy Norton were simply an audience; they played no active part in the unseen drama that was being enacted beyond their balcony.

Was either experience paranormal? Let us look at the facts again.

Miss Moberley and Miss Jourdain seem to have had no clear idea of what they would find at the Petit Trianon. They had some general knowledge of 18th-century French history and of Marie-Antoinette's life at Versailles, but their visit to the Queen's château at Versailles was prompted principally by the prospect of a pleasant walk through the gardens on a warm afternoon.

As soon as they approached the Petit Trianon, their pleasure was marred; their sightseeing trip became less attractive than they had anticipated. The two women felt oppressed and disorientated. They had difficulty in finding their way through the woods and among the paths. The strangeness of the people they encountered – the man at the kiosk, the unseen runners, the gentleman, the footman, the lady with the fichu – added to their unease. Their account of the events of that afternoon, although it was written three months later, conveys something of their disquiet. It is quite straightforward, almost naïve. Had they had any intention to deceive, to invent a plausible story or to perpetrate an elaborate fraud, they would surely have taken much greater care over both their research and their experience. Indeed, their innocence and the lack of expertise that is evident from their subsequent investigations are convincing proof of the women's sincerity. They were clearly hoping to make sense of what they had experienced and trying to interpret the facts they had discovered about the Petit Trianon and its history in a way that would accord with the places and the people they had seen that afternoon. In the light of modern psychical research, this was not a wise undertaking,

Above: the Belvédère, one of the ornamental buildings in the grounds of the Petit Trianon at Versailles, which had been built at the time of Marie-Antoinette. Critics of the alleged timeslip experienced by Misses Moberley and Jourdain have assumed that this was in fact the 'kiosk' they described. But on her return visit to Versailles in 1902, Miss Jourdain dismissed this theory. She took note of the Belvédère – but still insisted it was not the kiosk, which she could no longer find

but the Versailles episode happened at the turn of the century, when the techniques of psychical research were less sophisticated than they are now.

Miss Moberley's and Miss Jourdain's record of their experience may not have been meticulous enough to convince sceptics, but many critics fell into the common trap of producing counter-explanations less credible than that of paranormality. Some claimed, for example, that the women had merely seen 20th-century figures and had imagined that they belonged to an earlier period. But the topography of the gardens – the bridge and the waterfall, certain areas of woodland – was quite different from that of Versailles in 1901. How could the people have been contemporary if the background was not?

To turn to the experience of Agnes and Dorothy Norton at Puys: they too had brought with them on their holiday only the most general knowledge of the history of the area. Yet for three hours they stood on their balcony listening to the sounds of an invisible battle raging on the beach at Dieppe, the details of which generally matched other accounts of the famous raid in 1942. Their experience is not unique: other observers have encountered re-enactments of battles fought long ago. Until comparatively recently, the sights and sounds of Marston Moor, the bloody clash between Roundheads and Cavaliers in the English Civil War, were regularly heard and seen near the battlefield. The author knows of two people who have accidentally walked into other ancient skirmishes.

A sensitive issue

Critics made much of the discrepancies in the accounts of Dorothy and Agnes. They pointed out that the women had not mentioned the noises to each other when they first heard them, and they noted that the two women's records contained minor differences of chronology. However, two points should be noted in defence of the Nortons' accounts. First, it was Dorothy, and not Agnes, who was the acknowledged sensitive. Agnes may have acted as a medium, or channel, for Dorothy, and she may have been slower to respond to the stimulus of the sounds that had no apparent source. Second, no two people ever experience an event identically, particularly where an impression of time is involved. The accounts of two witnesses of any event rarely tally exactly.

There are more serious objections to be made to the Nortons' claim that their experience was paranormal. Critics have suggested several natural explanations for the noises they heard. The dredger at work in the harbour, for instance: was that the sound that disturbed them? The noise of a dredger is unmistakable: it is a regular, fluctuating sound, something between a groan and a drone. However, the noise is certainly not a 'roar', which is what Dorothy claimed she heard, and no dredger could reproduce the sounds of battle – 'gunfire', 'shellfire', 'dive-bombers', 'landing craft' and 'cries'. Once heard, the noise of dive-bombers is not forgotten. Landing craft, though? What noise do they produce that is identifiable, unambiguously, at a distance? This detail seemed to critics to be implausible – but it is possible that Agnes had become familiar with the noise when she was a member of the WRNS during the war. The noise of aircraft: was that simply the sound of civil airlines flying over Puys en route to Turin? Yet another sceptic suggested that the noise was produced by the abnormally high tide that washed over the beach at Puys that night – an unlikely explanation, since it would hardly account for the 'cries' and 'gunfire' of battle.

However, certain questions do remain

Left: the combined operations raid on Dieppe by the Allies on 19 August 1942, and the resulting devastation of the holiday resort of Dieppe (above). Fifty years almost to the day after the Versailles timeslip, Agnes and Dorothy Norton claimed that their French holiday was also interrupted by the past – this time by the 'unmistakable' sounds of the Allied invasion. Because their experience was entirely auditory a number of alternative – natural – explanations have been put forward. But no one will ever be sure that the Nortons did not, as they claimed, have the paranormal experience of hearing the battle nine years after it took place

unanswered. The Nortons claimed that at the very time they were listening to the sound of the battle on the beach, they were aware that the noises probably had a paranormal source. This is most unusual. One of the striking facts about psychical experiences is that those involved rarely recognise them as such until later. Subjects often have a sense of unease and bewilderment while the events are taking place, but this may be accounted for by the fact that they are receiving information from two sources simultaneously: the senses, which are restricted by the confines of chronological time, and a paranormal source, which is subject to no such constraint. Furthermore, the onset of psychical experience often appears to be associated with the alpha brainwave pattern, the brain's 'neutral' gear, when the subject is not concentrating on anything in particular. The act of bringing concentration to bear on a paranormal experience generally causes the alpha pattern to be replaced by another, which rouses the subject out of the state in which he is likely to experience psychic phenomena. If Agnes and Dorothy Norton realised that what they were hearing had a paranormal source, it is curious that they did not 'emerge' from the experience immediately.

There is one other issue that has remained unresolved. On 30 July, a few days before the night on which the two women heard the sounds of the raid on Dieppe, Dorothy was

The battle of Marston Moor, fought on 2 July 1644, the first major royalist defeat of the English Civil War. There have been several cases recorded of people in the area of Marston Moor (a few miles from York) suddenly finding themselves surrounded by the sights and/or sounds of this battle, much as the Nortons seem to have experienced the Dieppe landings

awoken by a similar noise. She did not mention this fact to her sister-in-law. Was that because she did not regard that experience as paranormal? If not, why did she and Agnes conclude that the sounds they heard together so soon afterwards had a paranormal source?

The experience of Miss Moberley and Miss Jourdain at Versailles appears to bear all the marks of a large-scale retrocognitive timeslip. The transposed landscape, the presence of people from another age, the exchanges that took place between the two 20th-century women and the people they met as they wandered through the woods and along the paths – all these suggest that for them time had become dislocated.

The Dieppe case is less clear-cut. It may have been a timeslip of a similar kind, though exclusively auditory and more restricted in scope. What throws doubt on the paranormality of the experience, curiously enough, is the additional detail supplied by Agnes, who provided a more precise record of what she had heard and who mentioned landing craft, in spite of the fact that it was Dorothy who was the psychic.

Is it ever possible to prove beyond doubt that an experience that revives past events is a paranormal one? It seems not, for even when several witnesses confirm a detailed account of the experience, someone is sure to suggest an hallucination or telepathy.

Why is it that certain areas of the world seem to be focal points for mysterious happenings? Are these 'window areas' gateways to another time? JENNY RANDLES discusses some examples

'IT HAS BEEN OBSERVED, on more than one occasion, that there exists [*sic*] peculiar haunted regions upon the face of this planet. These enigmatic "window areas", which serve as focal points for UFOs, mystery animals, and all manner of unusual phenomena, are often as puzzling as the "Things" they host.' So wrote American phenomenologist David Fideler as he opened a major survey of one such 'window', in Michigan, USA, for the magazine *Fortean Times*.

Windows, doorways, gateways or portals into the unknown have been talked about for a very long time. Local legend sometimes associates paranormal happenings with certain spots. Knowes, or Neolithic burial mounds, are often regarded as such magical places; one story tells of two Orkney fiddlers who were walking past a knowe when suddenly, in the middle of a sentence, one disappeared. Years later the remaining fiddler was passing the mound when suddenly his companion was back, his eye still as bright and his beard still as black as so many years before, and on his lips the end of the sentence he had been saying when he disappeared.

A favourite science-fiction theme is of the man who suddenly steps through a time or space warp into another world. The famous movie *2001 – a space odyssey* shows star travellers reaching their destination by such

Windows on another world?

Stonehenge, fascinating in the great antiquity that hides its origins from modern knowledge. Ancient sites like this are often associated with strange phenomena and events

A giant explosion whose cause was never explained occurred on 1 January 1970 at Pullman (below), a suburb of Chicago (left) on the shore of Lake Michigan. This, added to the many other reports of queer events in the region, has made the Michigan Anomaly Research Group study team believe that Lake Michigan is a window area

a route. Even modern music ensures that this concept remains in our consciousness. The rock group The Moody Blues had a hit with a song called *Slide zone*, describing the effects of falling through a window in the framework of space. So clearly this is a familiar idea. But just what evidence is there for the existence of such windows?

David Fideler is a member of the Michigan Anomaly Research Group, set up to investigate the window concept scientifically. Here is just one example of the kind of case the team has on its records. They believe it suggests that Lake Michigan constitutes a window area.

On 31 March 1897 a brilliant white light appeared in the sky over Galesburg. It was accompanied by a strange crackling sound.

Ten days later, fishermen at Pine Lake observed an 'alien' animal, something like a panther – panthers are not indigenous to Michigan. It made a 'terrible noise' and was blamed for the slaughter of local livestock.

On 6 February 1901, a mysterious fall of dust-like material descended inexplicably on Paw-Paw on a perfectly calm day.

In May 1954 a motorist at La Porte (a nicely synchronous French name that means 'the door') observed three oval UFOs that gave out beams of light. His car engine and radio failed while the UFOs flew by overhead.

Five years later, a young mother at Sister Lakes started a wave of sightings of gorilla-like 'furry' humanoids similar to the bigfoot or sasquatch.

On 1 January 1970 a gigantic explosion rocked Pullman at a quarter past midnight. Windows were broken, things fell from shelves, and a mysterious large hole appeared in

the frozen surface of a lake 200 yards (180 metres) from the shore, throwing great chunks of ice high into the air. The unexplained blast was felt 4 miles (7 kilometres) away.

Lastly, in August 1976 several witnesses at New Buffalo saw a misty white object floating over a field; it was interpreted by one witness as a ghost and by another as an angel.

All these, and many other weird experiences in the vicinity, imply that there may be something strange about the place. Sceptics may claim that *any* populated area would reveal a similar catalogue if researched thoroughly enough, but there is sufficient evidence to prove that certain areas record far more than their fair share of mysterious phenomena.

The Devil provides a clue

Etymological evidence sometimes provides a clue to the discovery of window areas. For if an area has always experienced a large number of strange events, this may be reflected in its name. Loren Coleman, an American writer on the paranormal, has conducted a study of what he calls 'Devil names', locations whose names contain 'Devil', or the equivalent in the local language. He theorises that these places often receive their names because of their reputation – for example, rumours of terrifying encounters would in ancient times have been directly linked with the Devil. Coleman analysed a large number of such places throughout the USA, and found that very often they were rich in a wide variety of peculiar events. He concluded: 'Geographical "Devil names", worldwide, may indicate . . . locales high in Fortean energy and strangeness. These places

'Light ball' phenomena have been reported at two localities in France – the town of Draguignan at the foot of Malmount hill (above) and the district of Aveyron (below). Such anomalous events are considered to be a strong characteristic of a window area

deserve some extra attention. . . .'

David Fideler concurs. He points to an area around Draguignan in France (the name is possibly derived from 'dragon') and a nearby hill, le Malmount, which translates into English as 'the evil mountain'. Several strange incidents are reported to have taken place there – including the appearance of mysterious floating balls of light, and the mountain-top confrontation between a car and humanoid figures that emerged from a 'glow'.

This kind of 'light ball' phenomenon is in fact the commonest occurrence in an apparent window area, and must be assumed to be important. The similarity to the rarely seen ball lightning is obvious. Ball lightning, however, occurs in certain well-defined meteorological conditions, whereas there appears to be no such restriction on when and where the window area light balls can appear. It seems fairly likely that the light balls, like ball lightning, are electrical effects; but, whereas ball lightning is caused by a static electrical charge in the atmosphere, light balls may be caused by a charge in the ground itself, produced by some kind of magnetic anomaly.

The catalogue of events at Aveyron in France is typical of experiences at a window area. François Lagarde was the author of an excellent study of this affair that appeared in *Flying Saucer Review* and the French UFO journal *Lumières dans la nuit*.

The story concerns an isolated farming family who had lived in the depths of the countryside for many years. On 15 June 1966 they saw a series of light balls, which were about 4 feet (1.2 metres) in diameter, floating about their large farmyard, climbing over hedges and seemingly inspecting things. They disappeared by 'blending into' a large

opaque vertical cylinder of light in a nearby field. Over the next few years, these light balls were seen frequently, the cylinder always appearing with them. It was on the night of 11 January 1967, however, that the family experienced what appears to have been the most bizarre phenomenon of all.

The farmer's son decided to take his car and pursue one of the light balls. He saw some of the balls blend into the cylinder, only one of them remaining outside it. As he approached the object, which was hovering above the road, his car lights and engine cut out. Desperately he tried to restart the car and turn on the internal light – but nothing happened. He had no power at all. He felt unable to move. Suddenly a small saucer-shaped object flew towards him, straight across the fields. It had two small domes on top, and inside, surrounded by a greenish haze, were two humanoid figures wearing green overalls. The UFO came closer, and then departed with a blast of heat. The metallic road sign close to him began to vibrate visibly as the UFO flew away. Eventually the witness recovered and was able to return home, but he suffered strange reactions for some time afterwards. At first he could not sleep; then he slept for 20 hours or more. He found himself floating as if out of his body; he also experienced temporary limb paralysis on several occasions.

Clearly these balls of light that seem so often to invade window areas are very odd things indeed – capable of inducing quite disturbing effects.

To return to Loren Coleman's link between 'Devil names' and strange occurrences. There are many 'Devil names' in Britain, although sometimes they are of a

Below: Devil's Garden, the scene of a frightening close encounter that took place on 27 January 1978. The secluded spot lives up to Loren Coleman's theory that place names with 'Devil' in them have a high incidence of weird occurrences

Bottom: Boggart Hole, Clough, is another of Britain's place names that indicate a history of mysterious encounters. 'Boggart' is a northern name for ghosts

local nature and not readily found on maps. Boggart Hole, Clough, in north Manchester, for example, is so named because of frequent meetings here with the 'boggarts' – a northern name for spirits or ghosts.

One of Britain's most frightening close encounter events took place at the Devil's Garden, a secluded spot beside the River Weaver, near Frodsham in Cheshire. The date was 27 January 1978. At 5.45 p.m. four men in their late teens were wandering through some meadows close to a weir. They had to admit that they were poaching, which meant that they were rather unwilling to discuss their story. But on this night they were to bag rather more than they had bargained for.

They saw a strange object floating along the surface of the river from the direction of Weaverham. It was about 20 feet (7 metres) above the ground, and at first they took it to be a satellite that was out of control (a Soviet satellite had crashed in Canada a few weeks earlier, so this was a natural assumption). The 'satellite', a round silvery object with a small skirt underneath, floated down into the nearby undergrowth, emitting flames as it did so. It sat there, immobile and eerie, making a sound like rushing wind.

The men were very scared, of course, but well hidden in the bushes, so they felt reasonably secure. They gazed in amazement as a peculiar bluish glow, which may have been ultra-violet light, emanated from the object; it hurt their eyes to stare at it. Just as they were about to run, with thoughts of radioactivity now uppermost in their minds, a 'man' appeared around the side of the object. He surveyed some cows in a nearby field, which were standing unnaturally still, perhaps through fright. A moment later, he went back round the craft and returned with a colleague; between them they carried a

what Keel has to say he undoubtedly means us to take very seriously indeed.

One window he claims to have found is in West Virginia. For months during 1967, local citizens were plagued by an horrific apparition, a winged humanoid creature that was dubbed 'Mothman'. There were also cold spots, space messages and meandering light balls. Warnings were received telepathically and from mysterious aliens that the current Middle East situation might escalate into a third world war, and that a nationwide power failure was imminent. Few people took any notice of these things, but Keel knew better. On 15 December 1967 he sat watching the television news, sure that *something* was about to happen.

Over in West Virginia, it was the busy evening rush hour. At Point Pleasant an old steel bridge carried the road across the Ohio River. Under the abnormal load of a traffic snarl-up it creaked and groaned, tottered and swayed. Then, suddenly, it snapped. Cars and screaming people were plunged to their doom. Bodies and wreckage floated on the icy surface as the night set in. Thirty-eight people were dead. Meanwhile, local residents who had been spared the disaster looked into the sky and saw, bobbing up and down above the river, meandering balls of light.

Point Pleasant was right in the middle of Keel's West Virginia window.

frame-like structure not unlike a cage.

The men wore silver suits and helmets that bore lamps. They placed the large frame-like structure, which appeared to be very light, around one of the cows, and proceeded to take measurements by moving some struts up and down. The four men had by now had enough and fled the scene, no doubt thinking that they might be next on the list for inspection, and not relishing the thought. They ran until they reached the village; one of them felt a strong 'pulling' sensation tugging him backwards by his genitals. These were sore for some days afterwards, and red as if sunburned – needless to say, this was out of the question in an English winter!

Macabre horror

Undoubtedly the major proponent of the window area theory is American journalist and collector of oddities John Keel. His restless pursuit of the myths and monsters, falling frogs and flying saucers that haunt his native land is pervaded by the wry humour that so characterised the writing of Charles Fort. But to read John Keel's work gives one a sense of macabre horror. It is hard to handle the idea of his characters being real, so it is comforting to think of them as roles for Vincent Price or Christopher Lee. But

Above: two silver-suited figures emerged from a shiny round object at the Devil's Garden in Cheshire and took measurements of a cow in the nearby meadow. They were seen by four youths, one of whom was left with a painful reminder of the close encounter

Right: the twisted wreck of the Silver Bridge at Point Pleasant in West Virginia, USA. On the night the bridge collapsed without a known cause, balls of light were seen in the sky

Through the glass—darkly

A spate of reports of strange phenomena centred on one location can quickly lead to the conclusion that a window area has been discovered. Some places are notorious for paranormal happenings and these are often where such legends develop

PERHAPS THE WORLD'S most famous window area is the Bermuda Triangle. Through the promotion of numerous writers, most notably Charles Berlitz, it has become widely known – and, if fame alone were a guide to the truth, this part of the Atlantic Ocean would be of enormous importance. Unfortunately it is not.

There are a growing number of serious students of the paranormal who suspect that the Bermuda Triangle is a gigantic myth, the product of distortion, exaggeration and a plain disregard for the facts. Books by Larry Kusche and Paul Begg, a contributor to *The Unexplained*, have cast considerable doubt on many of the classic cases on which the Triangle legend rests. So, one feels entitled to ask, is there any substance at all to the mystery?

As with all window area cases, this question is difficult to answer. Separating truth from rumour is a tricky, sometimes impossible business. But there are some stories that do at least intrigue, and may suggest that there is more to the notion than some people are prepared to admit. Here is one example, an account that was submitted in early 1981 to a British UFO research society, the UFO Investigators' Network (UFOIN), as a UFO report – although, as will become evident, this is a less than adequate description of its contents.

The story came from an elderly seaman, recently retired, who in the autumn of 1928 was a crewman aboard a large tanker. The ship was sailing the Atlantic, somewhere just east of Florida, in the course of a long voyage. At the time, of course, there was no talk of the Bermuda Triangle – the concept had not yet been invented. But it seems, nevertheless, that this is where the ship was situated.

One evening at about 8 p.m. the sailor was in his cabin, about to go to the ship's library as was his custom. Things seemed oddly quiet, so he went out on deck to investigate. He was disturbed by what he found: the ship was almost totally deserted! He walked the decks of the long, narrow tanker, surveying all the places where people should be. He found nothing. The entire crew seemed to have disappeared off the face of the Earth.

Not surprisingly, the man was a little distressed. His disquiet was not eased as he looked out over the rails towards the sea. For here, too, things were far from normal. The sea and sky seemed to blend into one at the horizon, forming a continuous flat, grey surface. The smooth monotony went on and on, giving no indication of motion or time. Above the horizon, or where the horizon should have been, there was a kind of leaden grey dome that towered in an arc across the bows of the ship. Whether part of the sky, or some hovering form, the man could not tell, but in later years pictures of domed UFOs reminded him of it. Except that if this *was* a UFO, it was gigantic – it occupied around 120° of arc!

In desperation, the sailor sat down on the deck, on a narrow walkway. Anyone passing along the ship had to come this way. After a few timeless minutes, without a clue where he was or what to do, the man was relieved to

Below: a seaman's terrifying experience aboard a tanker in the west Atlantic Ocean in 1928: for several minutes, the entire crew disappeared and what seemed to be a huge UFO filled the sky. The tanker was, it seems, then in the famous Bermuda Triangle region, once notorious, but now thoroughly discredited, as a dangerous window area

see one of his shipmates rush towards him, yelling 'Where have you been?' He told how the crew had begun looking for him when he had not turned up for his habitual visit to the library, and had apparently completely disappeared. They had scoured the ship for him, but found no trace. The sailor looked up to find the sea and sky normal once more, and the oppressive feeling of 'time suspension' no longer with him. He did not know what to say. For there was no way that even two people searching for one another on the ship could have avoided a meeting for 10 minutes or more. The walkway was not wide enough for two people to pass each other.

Of course, we can do no more than treat this as an interesting mystery story. What status it has as a factual account must remain open to doubt. But it does have close connections with other examples of time anomaly – it is as if, for a few minutes, two worlds diverged, as in the parallel universe theory of

Above right: Cradle Hill, Warminster, in southern England, scene of many of the UFO encounters and other weird events that have taken place in and around Warminster since Christmas Day 1964. Local journalist Arthur Shuttlewood (right) has done much to stimulate interest in the strange phenomena; the idea that they have some message for humankind has taken root in the minds of local inhabitants, as is shown by this graffito (far right) from Cradle Hill

time (see page 80), and the sailor jumped out of the time/space lane in which he was previously and subsequently travelling.

Perhaps this is indeed what happened, or perhaps there is a different explanation. Stories such as this are the skeletons upon which the Bermuda Triangle myth has been built and fattened up until unrecognisable, by writers who have one eye on the extraordinary human interest they possess, and another on the possible financial gain.

One of the greatest dangers in trying to locate window areas lies in relating things that really do not have any relationship at all.

Once a location is credited with mysterious powers, anything and everything can be made to fit in with this hypothesis. The process is illustrated by a purported UFO landing in Urmston, Greater Manchester, England. The object turned out to be nothing more than the planet Venus, blazing more brightly than usual in the early dawn sky – but to the media this explanation was of no interest. What did interest them was the version reported by the witnesses, where Venus became a mysterious flying saucer. Basing their theories on this biased interpretation, a whole host of people started to associate new phenomena with the 'UFO' and its 'landing site'. Indeed, by now even the light that was originally reported had grown in popular conception to a structured metal disc! Some horses in a field, moving about restlessly – in reality probably bothered by the freezing weather – came to be 'reacting to a force field generated by the object'. And one theorist even concluded that a mysterious epidemic of vanishing cats, lost over preceding months from a local estate, had in fact been abducted by the aliens!

'The Warminster Thing'

The most famous window area in Britain is undoubtedly Warminster, a quiet country town on the edge of Salisbury Plain. In late 1964 its peace was shattered by the arrival of what came to be known as 'the Warminster Thing'. The 'Thing' came in several guises – UFOs, balls of light, strange noises, weird animals and so on. Very soon the entire town was on the lookout for the 'Thing', which was for a time as famous as the Loch Ness monster. Warminster was suddenly *the* place to be if you wanted to see something unusual; indeed, people still flock there from all over the world to sit and talk to other 'believers' in the 'Thing', or to try to catch a fleeting glimpse of the wondrous visitor. Even the local graffiti tend to follow the trend: one wall bears a plea to the aliens, a sign of the frustration the passing years have brought – 'Go back to Venus. . . . We don't want your lies no more!'

What was it that made Warminster so special? Its fame began with a rumour that may well have been based on some real experiences. But the place became such an overnight sensation, and fiction became subtly mixed with fact to such an extent that it is impossible to gauge whether there really is something remarkable about the place. There are inevitable suspicions that much of what followed was the product of some kind of human need to believe in the supernatural, and therefore to see it. After having made a long pilgrimage to stand on one of Warminster's chilly hillsides, it would not be very difficult for someone to persuade himself that the lights of a distant helicopter just might be something a little more peculiar. And there are many army bases in the area that conduct all kinds of military manoeuvres

on the plain – tanks, aircraft and helicopters, often in unusual configurations, various kinds of flares and searchlights, are all familiar sights to Warminster residents. But to an outside observer who has come to see the 'Thing', they can prove very deceptive.

Over the years, the man who has been mainly responsible for keeping the Warminster mystery afloat has been a local journalist, Arthur Shuttlewood. It was he who first brought the enigma to the notice of the world in his best-selling book *The Warminster mystery*, and many others. He writes with a lively style that endears him to his readers; from all over the world he collects stories of what people have seen in and around Warminster, and he has a few strange tales of his own to tell. All this has ensured continued interest in the mystery, leading more and more people to come and see for themselves.

Some people allege that the military in the area take a special interest in the mystery. There are even claims that they harbour a stack of secret photographs. In the summer of 1981 a couple visiting Warminster for the first time waited on a hillside as dusk set in, and were astonished when a military helicopter came out of the gloom and hovered close above them, the co-pilot leaning right out of the cockpit and staring down at them – all this despite the fact that they were on private, not army, land. However, none of this proves anything. Military men are human, and like anyone else they could merely have a personal interest in the mystery, and not be acting under orders to investigate it.

The Warminster case does not stand alone. The same pattern has been repeated, usually on a somewhat smaller scale, in many other locations throughout the world. One of the common denominators seems to be the

Troops stage a mock 'section attack' (above), and helicopters manoeuvre (below) on training exercises. It is easy to see how perfectly routine exercises staged by the many army bases on Salisbury Plain, close to Warminster, could be misinterpreted by the unwary as apparitions of the Warminster 'Thing'

presence of a focal figure who collects the reports, such as Arthur Shuttlewood at Warminster or John Keel at Michigan (see page 53). Around them the mystery spins itself. Whether there is anything there to start with, or whether the mystery actually results from their interest in it, is a question that is often impossible to answer. Hilary Evans has analysed in detail how the mystery of the 'Welsh Triangle' of Dyfed, west Wales, was born during 1977. Here authors of popular books picked up a tiny thread and wove a complex tapestry of distortion, lies and half-truths – plus a few genuine puzzles.

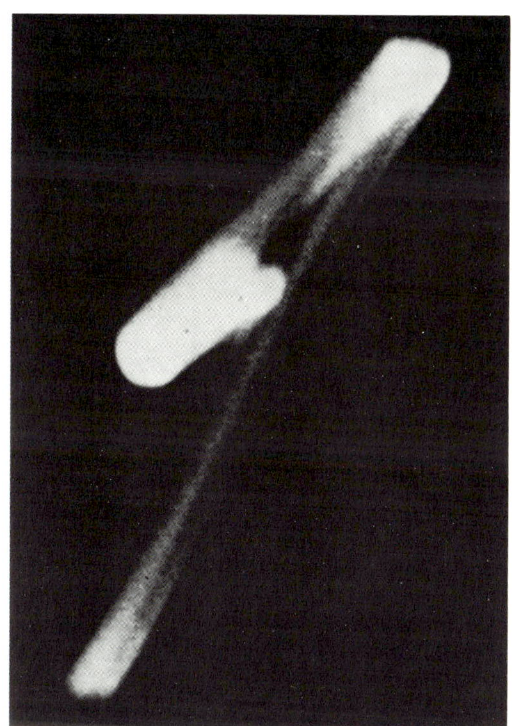

One might be tempted to conclude that window areas simply do not exist. Nevertheless, there is an amount of unimpeachable evidence that suggests that certain areas just might attract strange events. Perhaps one of the best cases is the mystery of the Clwyd area of north Wales.

Deluge of weird events

In the summer of 1976, three children of the Sunderland family independently claimed to have seen strange alien creatures and UFOs in fields near Oakenholt, a small village close to Flint, Clwyd. This report led to a deluge of weird events, enveloping the family in a sequence of weird happenings.

These events did not receive any wide attention in the press – but, while investigators were researching them, other people in the immediate vicinity came forward with stories that were strangely similar to those of the Sunderland family. One teenage girl was so terrified by her experiences that she refused to talk to anyone for days. The revelations prompted a search through the records of the local newspaper to see if any anomalous events had been reported in the past. Indeed they had! Over the previous 10 years there had been a number of stories of yellow balls of light similar to those seen by the Sunderland family, and anomalous figures of strange shapes. No one had attached much importance to these curiosities at the time, but now they lent considerable strength to the idea that the locality is, indeed, a window area. But what *is* a window area?

The area itself offered very few clues. It was true that it had ancient connections – there were plenty of old monuments and dykes, and the important Roman border city

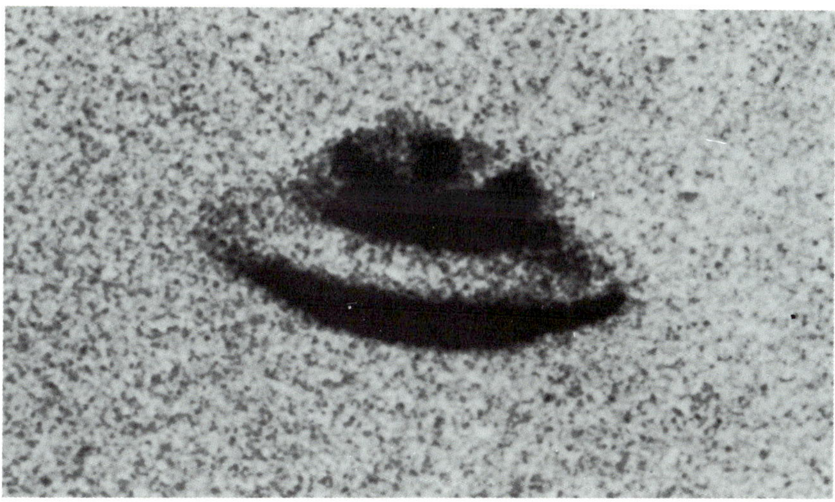

Two photographs of the Warminster 'Thing'. On 29 August 1965 it appeared as a classic UFO (above) and was photographed by 19-year-old factory worker Gordon Faulkner; on 2 January 1966 it shot across the sky as a glowing ball of light (above left), photographed by 15-year-old Bob Langley

Below: Gaynor and Darren Sunderland at the site near Flint, Clwyd, where they allegedly first saw alien beings and UFOs in 1976. Their report triggered a spate of sightings – and led to the suspicion that Flint was a window area

of Chester is nearby. There is also a major electricity grid supply station in the vicinity, a factor that has in some suspected window areas proved to be the cause of the appearance of strange phenomena. The area straddles the Dee estuary, a fact that may also be significant – the nearby presence of water is another factor that researchers have sometimes suggested might prove important.

Somewhere in the data may lie the reason for the phenomena. No one has yet found out for sure what window areas are, although there is certainly no shortage of ideas. These range from the mundane to the ridiculous, and include such possibilities as mini black holes, time warps and doors into another dimension. But gradually research has found itself settling onto one or two possibilities, and positive progress is at last being made.

Light through the window

A young couple, Caroline and Peter, who were renovating an old stone post office in the Cornish village of Newmill, came face to face with a luminous green and red object one night in 1977, which they later described as a 'UFO'. Almost immediately after the sighting they were both taken so ill that they had to be treated in hospital. Could their illness have been radiation sickness, induced by the effect of some form of natural radiation channelled through the stone of their house?

The existence of window areas has been hotly debated even by those interested in the paranormal – but there now seems to be some evidence for their authenticity, although the time warp theory is now in question

ARE WINDOW AREAS REAL? Many modern researchers would certainly argue that they are. Bernard Delair, a British UFO expert who works on the archives of Contact UK – the world's largest UFO society – has a working background in geography and has taken this problem very seriously. His own research began with a study of the temporal distribution of UFO 'flaps'.

Delair was able to identify two cycles, one of 10 to 11 years, and another of 4 to 6 years. Tracing these back into history, beyond the supposed beginning of the UFO phenomenon with Kenneth Arnold's 1947 sightings (see page 4), he found definite indications of a phenomenon that manifests itself in a cyclic fashion, being much commoner at certain times than at others. Further research that

Delair has carried out in conjunction with Ahmad Jamaludin has even revealed a geographical progression for these waves and explained some of their intricacies. Delair and Jamaludin believe that it is possible to predict where and when UFO activity will be strongest: in South America in 1982, in the central Americas in 1983 to 1984, in north America in 1985 and 1986, in northern Europe, possibly including Britain, in 1987, and in southern Europe in 1988. It will be interesting to see how many of these predictions turn out to have been accurate.

Delair has also carried out a mammoth survey of tens of thousands of reports recorded on computer files in the USA and Britain. His analysis of these reports led him to conclude that he could identify dozens of window areas in many countries.

The attempt to establish scientifically that window areas exist goes on. But if they *do* exist, what are they? Is a window area generated by the physical features of the region itself, or does the region attract some outside force? It seems that the first theory is more likely to be true. Delair has not missed the correlation between his primary wave cycle – 10 to 11 years – and the cycle of maxima and minima in sunspot activity. In fact, his comparison shows that the occurrence of these two things matches so closely that one is led to conclude that there must be some connection between sunspot activity and peaks and troughs in the occurrence of paranormal phenomena, especially UFOs.

Analysis of UFO flaps can tell us still more. The French scientist Dr Claude Poher decided to look at the reports during the big French flap of 1954. He compared the varying declination of the Earth's magnetic field with the number of UFO reports. The resultant graph leaves little doubt that there is a correlation. It seems that UFO activity and geomagnetic disturbance are linked.

Poher discovered one more important point. Forty per cent of the cases in this flap occurred within 1100 yards (1 kilometre) of a fault zone – a part of the Earth where the subsurface rocks are impacted against one another. Indeed, fully 20 per cent occurred *on* fault lines. This could be a highly significant finding; it has been confirmed in a study of the Spanish flap of 1968. A similar result has been obtained by researchers on the Dragon Project in England, who have found that almost all megalithic sites in the British Isles are within 1 mile (1.6 kilometres) of a fault line.

Magnetic attractions

Meanwhile, in Canada, two researchers, Michael Persinger and Ghislaine Lafrenière, have gone beyond the study of simple UFO reports. They have correlated many different kinds of anomaly with variations in the electromagnetic field strength. They feel confident that this demonstrates not only the validity of the window area concept, but also its relationship with electromagnetic radiation.

One of their proposals is of particular interest. They suggest that underground at window area sites there may be bodies of highly conductive material buried in the rock strata. During increased solar activity this normally dormant mass could, they claim, become electrically charged and generate a large electromagnetic field around it. This would account for the geomagnetic deviations, and the field would also be detectable at the surface. This massive 'superfield', they suggest, could have the strength to generate luminous effects in the atmosphere – the balls of light so common at window areas – and more peculiar effects in individuals who happen to be in the area when the superfield is active.

It is known that messages are carried in the brain by means of electrical impulses, and it is quite possible that contact with an intense superfield could cause some people to experience a kind of 'brain scrambling'

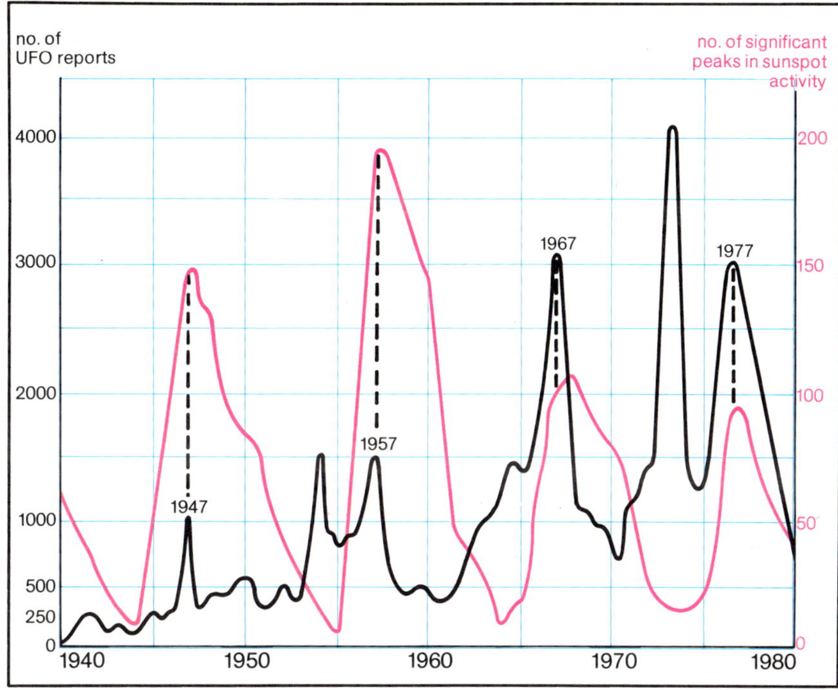

Top: a graph showing the correlation between sunspot activity and UFO 'flaps', as proposed by British UFO researcher Bernard Delair (above). Only the years 1940 to 1980 are shown, but the peaks in UFO activity since 1700 seem to occur every 10.2 years, while the sunspot cycle averages 10 to 11 years. According to this theory the next UFO flap in Europe should occur in 1988

– electrical interference that could result in hallucinations. It is believed that certain forms of electromagnetic radiation can be 'heard' inside the head as a humming or buzzing sound. Is it mere coincidence that humming is the sound, usually on the threshold of audibility, that is most often associated by witnesses with the onset of a paranormal experience? Electromagnetic fields can also produce subsidiary effects such as malfunction of electrical equipment, overtiredness and headaches or nausea. It is interesting to consider all this in the light of the following example.

During September 1977 a young couple, Peter and Caroline, were renovating a post office in the Cornish village of Newmill. One evening, Caroline went outside and came face to face with a luminous green and red object about 6 feet (2 metres) in diameter. She called Peter, and they both saw the object float up the ramp of a barn behind the house and zig-zag across a field. It then drifted across the moors, coming to rest about a mile (1.6 kilometres) away, where it stayed for some hours – and was witnessed by around 30 people. The following evening, four similar objects appeared. They were again witnessed by several people.

Both Caroline and Peter subsequently had to be treated in hospital. They had stomach pains, headaches and nausea. No cause was found for this mystery illness, which seemed to be in some ways similar to radiation sickness; after a week it disappeared of its own accord.

It is possible that a massive rock body under the surface may have been responsible for the light ball effect in the atmosphere. The stonework of the old post office could even have channelled this effect as a lightning conductor attracts lightning. Close contact between witnesses and the ball of light may have induced the illness through possible attendant microwave radiations. It is interesting to note that others who saw the object from a greater distance apparently suffered no ill effects.

This case suggests ways in which a superfield could affect the brain. The ball of light, although itself real, could become the starting point of a complex hallucination, stimulated by the intense radiation of the superfield. If the superfield led the electric channels of the brain to overload temporarily and 'short circuit', thus causing the conscious brain to 'switch off', hallucinations experienced during the subsequent period of unconsciousness might be triggered by the sensory input being given to the brain immediately preceding loss of consciousness. And so the brain might spin a fantasy around this sensory input and its own stored knowledge of UFOs. If the witness does not interpret what he sees immediately before losing consciousness as a UFO, or if indeed he sees nothing, then the resultant fantasy could take any form, and would probably be associated with his own personal beliefs or fears, or whatever he happened to be thinking about just before the superfield struck. If such a loss of consciousness were fairly short and the witness had no previous experience of

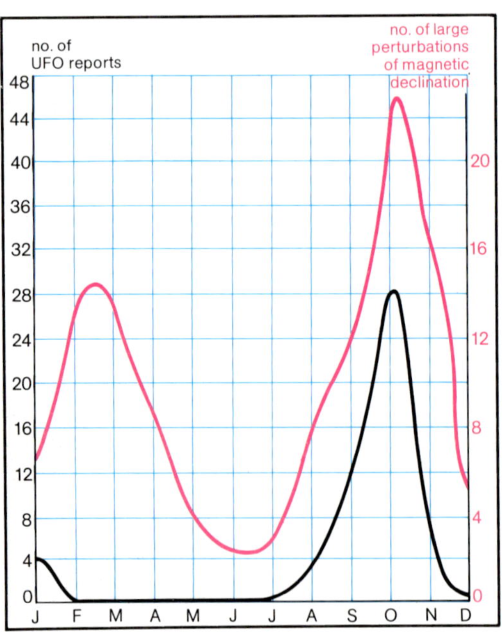

blackouts, he might regard the intermediary dream or hallucination as real.

Some researchers believe they can explain *all* visionary experiences in this way. Some light may be thrown on the matter by study of the medical condition known as epilepsy. This is a temporary 'brainstorm' during which the sufferer loses consciousness for a short time and can continue afterwards not realising he has had an attack. The interesting thing is that hallucinatory dreams are a feature of epileptic blackout periods. Perhaps the superfield leads to a kind of mass

Left: a graph showing the correlation between the French 'humanoid' flap of 1954 (above: Marius Dewilde, who had a famous close encounter of the third kind in 1954, seen outside his home at Quarouble) and the incidence of magnetic storms. This analysis was the work of the French scientist Dr Claude Poher, who also discovered that 40 per cent of the sightings during the flap occurred within 1100 yards (1 kilometre) of a geological fault zone – and 20 per cent actually on a fault line. Does close proximity to these areas at certain times induce hallucinations – of UFOs, ghosts and other paranormal phenomena?

'super epilepsy' in which large numbers of people suffer the same hallucination. While some witnesses of window area phenomena do not suffer hallucinations but *do* see some of the attendant phenomena, such as balls of light, and may also suffer physical side effects, others become unconscious. Time loss appears to be an important feature of UFO contact experiences, and time loss would of course occur if a blackout period were missing from conscious recall.

Earthquake lights

Another possibility is that window area phenomena are produced directly by the movement of rocks under the Earth's surface. This work took on a new importance when the findings of a group of scientists in Canada and the USA were released during early 1981. They had examined the piezoelectric effect, in which pressure or tension applied to certain types of crystal, such as quartz, induces an electrical potential. They suggested that stresses in the quartz crystals of certain types of rock might induce electrical activity in the surrounding atmosphere when the rock was under strain, as in Earth movements. Ionisation effects might even be visible as glowing light, rather like a UFO. The scientists decided to test this remarkable idea in the laboratory and found that they could indeed duplicate it. It does seem possible, therefore, that in a laboratory the size of the Earth the effect could be large enough to create realistic UFOs in the skies above fault zones. Indeed, what are known as

while Britain is geologically rather inactive, two of the major fault zones, where earthquakes are most likely to occur, cut across Loch Ness in Scotland and Stoke-on-Trent in central England. Loch Ness is host to many weird phenomena quite apart from its monster, and Stoke has for some years been the centre of an inexplicably high number of UFO close encounters. But perhaps the piezoelectric superfield theory in some way holds the answer.

The window opens wider

There are many possible consequences of this intriguing idea, not least the wealth of experiments it suggests. In the paranormal world, rigorous scientific experiment is all too rare, and serious researchers will be grateful for the chance this theory offers for scientific testing. Some students of leys have also been intrigued by the idea, and have attempted to measure electrical effects at megalithic sites; notable research has been carried out in England by workers in the Dragon Project at the Rollright circle in Oxfordshire.

It could be that these electromagnetic anomalies can also explain some curious photographic results that some researchers have obtained at megalithic sites and window areas. Using a type of infra-red film they have from time to time obtained unusual light effects and strange images, although nothing was visible to the naked eye on these occasions. It seems that the images were detectable only in the infra-red part of the spectrum – but it could be said that these pictures are further scientific evidence for the superfield.

It does seem that, if window areas really do exist, the concept of the superfield may offer a plausible working hypothesis on which to base investigations of the paranormal world.

Above: the scene of the Newmill sighting and (below) Laviano, Italy, which was completely destroyed by an earthquake in 1980. Do they represent two aspects of the same natural effect that in one case releases electromagnetic radiation (seen as a 'UFO') and in the other rips apart the Earth's surface?

'earthquake lights' have been reported immediately prior to a number of both major and minor Earth movements.

Already this theory has been invoked as a possible explanation for the mystery lights seen and photographed by a television crew over Kaikoura in New Zealand in December 1978. This area has a high incidence of Earth movements.

If this theory is to be acceptable, it should be possible to use it to predict the location of window areas. It is interesting to note that,

Psychics and scientists agree that we can explain the physical world only if we are prepared to jettison many of our common-sense ideas about the nature of time. What are these ideas, and why do we cling to them so tenaciously? ARCHIE ROY explores the issues

TIME – fleeting, phantom, ephemeral time – is truly the last frontier in its essential mystery, and an eternal fascination to men and women of all ages, a remorseless stream hurrying them onwards, freezing in the icebergs of the past their deeds, their triumphs, their follies. It wrenches from them their loved ones, it bears them towards the chilly mists of the fearsome future.

Prisoners on the ship of life, signed on for the duration of the voyage, we are conscious of the changing scenes, recording in our memories those that have gone, anticipating, predicting, attempting to plan the ship's course, trying to avoid foreseen reefs, steering for comfortable ports – yet knowing that the inexorable power of the current of time will always bear us on willy-nilly. We have no anchors strong enough to hold us upstream against the current. Time, as the hymn writer Isaac Watts truly said, like an ever-rolling stream bears all its sons away.

All living creatures have their biological clocks to measure time's passage – some crude like the promptings of hunger, some precisely attuned to the cycles of nature. Man possesses an additional gift, his mysterious consciousness, his ego, which can contemplate his existence, scan past memories and extrapolate from them, his ability to map mentally his position in the temporal and spatial environment, his restless curiosity spurring him on to explore his Universe.

From the time when Man's intelligence first took him beyond instinctive behaviour, he has been fascinated by time and its effects on the world around him. He witnessed the passage of the Sun across the sky and the slow yearly oscillation of its sunrise and sunset points against the eastern and western horizons. Linked to these cycles was his experience of the variable heat and brightness of day, the changing seasons and the migrations of animals. When the Sun spent a long time above the horizon the days were hot and the growth of living things was strong; when the day's duration was at its shortest, nature was frozen, bitter winds blew, and sleep, death's little brother, clasped many of the animals in his arms.

At night Man saw the Moon imitate with impatient speed the Sun's risings and settings. He observed the strange sequence of the lunar cycle, and the concept of the month was born. And the coast-dweller and fisherman discovered the even stranger link between the Moon's phases and the spring and neap high tides.

Below: a British beech wood photographed in spring, summer, autumn and winter. The mysterious cycles of nature, the procession of the seasons, the waxing and waning of the Moon and the orderly movement of the heavens, all led Man to assume that time moved steadily on, with events crystallising out of the unknown future into the present, and slipping into the unreachable past

All the mysterious cycles of the natural world seemed to be governed by the movements of the heavenly bodies. But the stars themselves were immutable, cold, remote diamond chips of light scattered in prodigal profusion at the beginning of time by some creator God across the invisible bowl of night, forever ordained to maintain their patterns while the bowl itself revolved, carrying them from rising to setting. A few, a very few stars – the planets – seemed freer than the rest, wandering at erratic speeds through the fields of space, occasionally stopping as if in contemplation of some cosmic dream, sometimes retracing their

time

Above: *The stages of life*, by Caspar David Friedrich (1774–1840). The human figures represent the ages of Man; the ships are symbols of our voyage through life

Above right: time-lapse photography reveals the growth of a winter aconite. Such changes in the natural world are sure signs that time is passing – but what clues do they give us to the nature of time itself?

steps in a seemingly purposeful manner for weeks or months on end before resuming their former progress.

Change, always change – birth and growth and decay and death. The baby became the little boy playing with toys, with his pets, with his playmates. The boy disappeared as the youth formed; his personality altered, his former life as baby and boy became memories, faulty, fleeting. The youth became a man; time flew past, bringing with it good harvests and bad, friends and enemies, old age and its infirmities. And always change. The impression forced upon Man by nature was one of time passing, of experiences presenting themselves to him in succession, forming out of the unpredictable and non-existent *future*, crystallising in the real and present *now* before slipping from his grasp into the fixed *past*. And as a further ironical trick of time, as he grew older, so did time seem to speed up, so that the endless summers of childhood gave way to the ever swifter passage of the seasons in old age.

> For when I was a babe and wept and
>   slept, Time crept;
> When I was a boy and laughed and
>   talked, Time walked;
> Then when the years saw me a man,
>   Time ran,
> But as I older grew, Time flew.

'If only I had my time over again'; 'If I only knew what awaited me'; 'I fear the future'; 'Why cannot this moment last forever?'; 'If I knew then what I know now'. The multitudinous cries of common Man echo the rueful tributes of poet, playwright and philosopher to the sovereignty of time passing.

In the Bible, in the book of Ecclesiastes (3: 1–2), we read:

> To every thing there is a season, and a time to every purpose under the heaven. A time to be born, and a time to die; a time to plant, and a time to pluck up that which is planted.

Much later, writing in the second century AD, the philosopher emperor Marcus Aurelius Antoninus muses:

> Time is like a river made up of the events which happen, and its current is strong; no sooner does anything appear than it is swept away, and another comes in its place, and will be swept away too.

The unstoppable flow of time bringing retribution terrifies the Dr Faustus of Christopher Marlowe (1564–1593):

> Now hast thou but one bare hour to
>   live,
> And then thou must be damned
>   perpetually;

Stand still, you ever-moving spheres
    of heaven,
That time may cease, and midnight
    never come.
The receding past provokes Shakespeare's
Richard II to cry: 'O! call back yesterday, bid
time return.'

Like so many poets of his time, Shakespeare was fascinated by the ruthless destruction produced by the passage of time.
Again and again in his sonnets and plays he
returns to the theme:
    When I have seen by Time's fell
        hand defaced,
    The rich-proud cost of outworn
        buried age.
In the *Rape of Lucrece* he writes:
    Mis-shapen Time, copesmate of ugly
        Night,
    Swift subtle post, carrier of grisly
        care,
    Eater of youth, false slave to false
        delight,
    Base watch of woes, sin's pack-horse,
        virtue's snare,
    Thou nursest all and murder'st all
        that are:
    O, hear me then, injurious, shifting
        Time!
    Be guilty of my death, since of my
        crime.
And there are the famous words of the
doomed Macbeth:
    To-morrow, and to-morrow, and to-
        morrow,
    Creeps in this petty pace from day to
        day,
    To the last syllable of recorded time;

Above left: Mephistopheles
drags Faust off to hell, in an
illustration by Willy Pogany.
'Stand still, you ever-moving
spheres of heaven,/That time
may cease, and midnight
never come,' says Faust,
knowing that this cannot
happen and that his
damnation at midnight is a
certainty

Left: a 19th-century
engraving showing the seven
ages of Man, by William
Mulready. Interpretations of
this subject, popular from the
15th to the early 19th
century, tended to give a
depressing picture of Man's
life as 'nasty, brutish and
short'

And all our yesterdays have lighted fools
The way to dusty death. Out, out, brief candle!
Life's but a walking shadow, a poor player
That struts and frets his hour upon the stage,
And then is heard no more.

This acknowledgement of the pathetic and momentary nature of Man's life is echoed by Sir Thomas Browne (1605–1682): 'The night of time far surpasseth the day.'

Herbert Spencer (1820–1903) defines time ironically: 'Time: that which man is always trying to kill, but which ends in killing him.'

Time dominates all Man's actions, emotions and desires. He cries out against time, which hurries him past joyous experiences; he equally fruitlessly protests at its laggard pace in his boredom, pain or misery. But time heeds him not. At its own pace it bears him along like a dog subservient to its master's plan.

The Concise Oxford Dictionary has a whole page of entries on time. Very few other topics take up this amount of space. And yet the direct number of words allocated to the definition of 'time' totals 12: 'Duration, continued existence; progress of this viewed as affecting persons or things'. Not, one must admit, a definition that provides much in the way of enlightenment regarding the nature of time. Our understanding of such an important subject seems minimal. And yet in every generation, there have been men and women who have given their best efforts in wrestling

Sir Thomas Browne (1605–1682), the famous thinker who, in his *Garden of Cyrus*, remarked, 'The night of time far surpasseth the day,' adding 'and who knows when was the equinox?'

with the subject, each seeking an understanding of the nature of time. For some time is an illusion, for others it is a linear process, a convenient mathematical or dynamical device; some have been forced to the conclusion that time is multi-dimensional; modern physicists have introduced the concept of the 'block Universe' in which time is but one dimension of a four-dimensional static, unchanging Universe explored by our individual consciousnesses. The theory of relativity has put elasticity into time: it flows at different rates in different places. The findings of 20th century quantum mechanics and nuclear physics have led some to conceive of even stranger universes in which time, if it passes, may even, for some subatomic particles, reverse its direction of flow.

Some of the most fascinating insights into the nature of time come from consideration of events best described as paranormal. Among these events are premonitions, precognitions and retrocognitions, apparitions spontaneous and experimental – events, in short, that many people are apt to dismiss as harmless lunacies, a legacy from our prescientific superstitious past, unworthy of the attention of any scientist. And yet it seems that, far from being deceitful or useless, these reports, and the analyses made of them by hard-headed philosophers and scientists, do indeed shed light on the anatomy of time, enabling us to come to certain important conclusions not only about its nature but also about the nature of the human personality.

Plus ça change...

The concept of time that has characterised the Western outlook on the world has always been a dynamic one. It was expressed in perhaps its most extreme form in the thought of the Greek philosopher Heraclitus (*c*.540–*c*.480 BC) – 'All things flow, nothing stays still'; 'Nothing endures but change.'

The importance assigned to time and change in Eastern thought results in a world view that is startlingly different. In Indian thought, in particular, time is conceived of as static rather than dynamic; the universal is emphasised at the expense of the changing, the particular: 'The one remains, the many change and flee.' Indian thought does not admit Heraclitus's contention that 'it is not possible to step in the same river twice': what is important is not the flow of water but the unchanging universal aspect of the river itself, a view closely echoed in Maurice de Macmahon's famous phrase 'Plus ça change, plus c'est la même chose' –

'The more things change, the more they stay the same.'

This static concept of the world is strongly reflected in the classical Sanskrit of ancient manuscripts (left). Sanskrit uses few descriptive verbs to denote action – 'John ran down the street', for example, becomes 'John did running down the street', in which 'running down the street' is regarded as a state in which John happened to be, rather than an action he chose to perform. Similarly, 'Because of the rain, the crops flourish' becomes 'Because of the rain, flourishing of the crops.' Heraclitus's 'All things flow' is almost unrecognisable as *sarvam anityam*, 'All existences are impermanent.'

This attitude to time results, in modern Hindustani, in linguistic features that can be confusing. *Kal* means both 'yesterday' and 'tomorrow'; *parson* means both 'the day after tomorrow' and 'the day before yesterday'. The real meaning of these words can be determined only by analysing the context in which they occur.

The waiting future

Premonitions and their counterparts, retrocognitions – the paranormal acquisition of knowledge about past events – are well-established psychic phenomena. What can they teach us about the nature of time?

THE COMMON-SENSE VIEW OF TIME is to split it into a past, which has gone, a future, which has not yet arrived and therefore does not exist, and a present moment, which is our only reality. But even a moment's thought reveals how complex, even contradictory, this seemingly simple notion is. For example, if we ask how 'thick' the present moment is we come to totally nonsensical answers. Is it a millisecond thick, or a nanosecond (one thousand millionth of a second), or is it even a picosecond (one thousandth of a nanosecond) thick? In thinking in this way it is worth noting that a picosecond in relation to a second is the equivalent of a second to 30,000 years! If we continue in this way, we are in danger of causing the whole Universe to vanish into absurdity.

In psychical research it is widely accepted that one royal road to our understanding of the nature of time, and probably also of the nature of human personality, is the study of cases of alleged precognition and retrocognition. Precognition is the paranormal acquisition of information about a future event.

That future event may be hours, days or even years ahead in time of the moment at which the precognition takes place. The word 'premonition' is often used to refer to precognition of a future disaster, either personal or public. It should be pointed out that we often obtain information, quite normally, about future events by a process of examination of present trends and knowledge of the laws governing these trends. Thus in the *Astronomical Almanac* there are listed future positions of Sun, Moon, planets and stars – but these are not precognitions. These future events are inferred from past knowledge and are not therefore precognitively predicted. Similarly, we may define a 'retrocognition' as the paranormal acquisition of information about a past event or scene – information that could not have been obtained from records, photographs or accounts of the event.

If one studies the proceedings and journals of societies for psychical research, the cases of ostensible precognitions and retrocognitions may persuade one that both do occur. Some cases are stronger than others;

Time and time again

One of the pioneers of modern research into time was J. W. Dunne (below right), whose books, some easy to read, others of the most mind-boggling difficulty, were published in the 1920s and 1930s.

Dunne's interest in time stemmed from some dreams he had while serving as a soldier in the Boer War. He sometimes dreamed of great disasters that subsequently happened in real life – and dreamed in such detail that if the dream had happened *after* the event, he would have assumed that the event caused the dream. But the dreams *preceded* the events. On 8 May 1902, the volcano at Mount Pelée on the island of Martinique erupted. Dunne dreamed of it beforehand – though, curiously, he later came to the conclusion that he had actually dreamed, not of participating in the disaster itself, but of reading the *Daily Telegraph* report of it (above).

Dunne concluded that such dreams were genuine experiences of events, but somehow *displaced in time*. He set out to develop a theory of time that would allow

for this weird phenomenon.

He began with the familiar concept of the block Universe. 'Now' is a slice of this Universe perceived by the self – called by Dunne 'Observer 1'. As time passes, Observer 1 experiences successive slices of the Universe. So far so good. But Dunne's master stroke was to introduce a 'Time 2' to measure the progress of Observer 1 through time, and a corresponding Observer 2, who follows slavishly Observer 1's waking progress but who, when Observer 1 is asleep, is free to range over the whole of Observer 1's life – past, present and future. This hypothesis led Dunne to postulate an infinite regression of times and observers analogous to the regression in Dunne's

some seem to involve information about great natural disasters such as earthquakes, tidal waves and volcanic eruptions, while others appear to relate to man-made catastrophes such as wars and revolutions, train, aeroplane and ship disasters. Many cases seem to refer to disastrous and tragic events that take place in the lives of the percipient and his immediate relations. With some psychics, prediction appears to be habitual – Edgar Cayce, Jeane Dixon, Eva Hellström, Gerard Croiset and Alan Vaughan. There are also occasional predictors, ordinary people who experience one or only a few premonitions of family or personal tragedies or even – seemingly pointlessly – trivial events of their day-to-day lives.

Future disasters

The clarity with which a person foresees a future disaster varies. One may speculate that it may be dictated not only by the strength of the subject's psychic ability, but also by the magnitude of the catastrophe. This may not be directly proportional to the number of people killed or injured; a single death can have far-reaching and unforgettable effects. Many people, even today, can remember the deep emotions aroused by news of the assassination of John F. Kennedy in Dallas in 1963 in addition to the exact circumstances in which they heard the news.

A remarkable collection of alleged premonitions of the Aberfan disaster was made by Dr J. C. Barker, a psychiatrist and a keen student of psychical phenomena for many

Above: scenes of confusion as emergency workers clear rubble after the Aberfan disaster of 1966. A study of premonitions of the catastrophe showed that there had been a clear 'pre-disaster syndrome' in which many people had felt a growing sense of unease as the event drew nearer. Psychiatrist Dr J. C. Barker has suggested that some people act as seismographs across time, picking up signs of events still distant in the future

years. Following his appeal for premonitions of the disaster, he received 76 letters and managed, after thorough investigation, to confirm 24 cases. When pieced together, the details of the premonitions provided a complete blueprint of the disaster – including the name of the village, that the disaster involved the collapse of a huge coaltip and that it would kill many children by enveloping a school so that they suffocated. A remarkable feature of the premonitions was that many of the people experiencing them felt various degrees of unease for varying periods of time before the event. Barker termed this constellation of premonitions the 'pre-disaster syndrome' and concluded that some human beings act like seismographs across time, with an extraordinary sensitivity to future disasters. The parapsychologist J. Gaither Pratt has suggested that such individuals are at least as common as left-handed people.

One such 'human seismograph' was the Marquis of Cazotte, a fellow of the Society of French Academicians who, at a dinner of the society held four years before the height of the Terror, startled his fellow guests by making a remarkably detailed prophecy of their fates. The prophecy was recorded by the French writer Jean-François de La Harpe. In turn, the Marquis told each one of the guests how they would die – by the guillotine or by slashing their wrists to avoid execution. The Marquis forecast that La Harpe would die a Christian. La Harpe was a confirmed free-thinker, and at this point one of his fellow academicians laughed and said, 'All my fears are now gone, for if we have to wait until La Harpe becomes a Christian then we shall live forever!' Although this story was not published until after the Revolution, reliable witnesses swore it *did* take place before the Terror, and

picture of himself painting himself (below).

Although Dunne's metaphysical arguments were flawed, his work remains an important pioneering study of the nature of time. His experimental findings that precognitive data enter our dreams have been confirmed by later researchers such as Montague Ullman and Stanley Krippner.

there is some evidence that the tale was known before 1789. If so, it was a remarkable prophecy – for it was accurate in every respect.

At the second international conference of the Society for Psychical Research, held at Trinity College, Cambridge, in March 1978, Professor Hans Bender read a paper describing a prophecy of war that far outdoes the Cazotte vision in its wealth of detail, as well as apparently describing events further away in the future.

In a letter to his family written in 1914, a Bavarian soldier on active service related the strange story of the prophecy of a French prisoner of war. The tone of the letter is jocular and sceptical, as indeed is understandable, for the Frenchman had some curious advice for his captors:

> They should throw away their guns because the war would end with defeat for Germany and her allies. After the war all Germans would become millionaires but they would throw their money from their windows and no one would pick it up because it would be worthless. In 1932 a man would come from the lower ranks to rule Germany and make preparations for a new war. This war, beginning in 1939, Germany would also lose although Italy would enter the war on Germany's side and many German soldiers would die in Italy. In 1945 Germany would be crushed from all sides and split up. The man and his sign would disappear.

In his book *Telepathy and clairvoyance*, the famous Dutch parapsychologist Professor W.H.C. Tenhaeff relates two examples of war predictions from his collection of such cases. In 1929, a Mrs W.R. and her family were visited by one of the sensitives studied

Above: the Marquis of Cazotte predicts the death of his companions in the French Revolution at a dinner held some years before the height of the Terror. The predictions were all, apparently, accurate – and the story, if true, is a powerful piece of evidence for precognition

Right: piles of banknotes made almost worthless by inflation in the Germany of the early 1930s. A Frenchman captured by German soldiers in 1914 had prophesied that after the First World War 'all Germans would become millionaires but they would throw their money from their windows and no one would pick it up because it was worthless'

by Professor Tenhaeff at their home on the Graaf Ottolaan at Oosterbeek near Arnhem. The sensitive became very upset and confessed that he had visions of all kinds of murder and manslaughter. He also heard ghastly sounds. He saw soldiers in uniform, of a kind he did not know, standing huddled over something like an Ordnance Survey map. He begged Mrs W.R.'s. husband to flee from the house and take everything they owned to safety. In 1944 the fighting in the vicinity was horrifying when the town of Arnhem became the scene of the heroic battle of a division of Allied paratroopers against the Germans. Some of the fiercest fighting took place in and around the houses in that area.

The second case concerned a Mr L.L., who had a recurring dream in which he seemed to be amid a body of men, all in civilian clothes, and yet they seemed to be standing in formation and obeying military commands. There were a large number of details that showed the dreamer that, although he had been in the army, it was not an

army experience that he was recalling in his dreams. Many years later, while he was in Indonesia, he was captured by the Japanese. Interned by them in a camp, he found himself going through the exact events that he had repeatedly dreamed of over the years. Interestingly enough, the dream never again came back after his return to Europe.

The sinking of the liner *Titanic* in April 1912 was an event that created in many the same harrowing emotions of loss, horror, agony and shock experienced half a century later after the Aberfan tragedy. The great liner, widely believed to be unsinkable, sailed on its maiden voyage carrying within it a representative sample of Western civilisation from all classes. Steaming at full speed through the night of 14 April, at 11.40 p.m. it struck an iceberg that ripped the ship's hull below the waterline.

Professor Ian Stevenson, who collected reports of a number of alleged paranormal phenomena connected with the sinking of the *Titanic*, has also suggested that such a disaster may produce psychic shocks by its very unexpectedness. Of Stevenson's 19 cases, 10 were precognitive.

Thresholds of consciousness

In a remarkable study carried out in the 1970s, W.G. Cox examined the theory that, although premonitions of a future disaster may never reach the conscious mind in a recognisable form, it may be strong enough to influence a person's behaviour. Cox selected a number of railway passenger trains involved in major accidents, and obtained data regarding the number of passengers on each train and the total number on the same train on the same run on previous occasions. Analysis of Cox's data suggests that some precognitions of misfortune may be sufficiently strong to cause changes of mind or cancellations without crossing the threshold of consciousness as a full blown premonition. Other investigators have collected numerous examples of cases where a premonition has reached a conscious level without any specified detail being attached to it. Dr Louisa Rhine gives the following example.

> My father was a manufacturer of washing machines and twice a year he would made a trip to the wholesalers and sell them a car load or two of washing machines. He saw dealers in Koekuk and was to take the 10 p.m. train for Davenport. He went to the depot, bought his ticket and then had a feeling that he should not go. It was so strong that he went back to the hotel and stayed in Koekuk overnight. In the morning when eating his breakfast he looked over the paper and found that the train he was supposed to have taken had been wrecked and nearly all the passengers in the smoker were killed. Dad was an

Above: an impression by artist David Shepherd of the disastrous battle of Arnhem in 1944. In 1929 a psychic visiting a family who lived near Arnhem experienced a vivid vision of the events of the battle, and became so distressed that he begged the family to leave the area

inveterate smoker.

If the future events in some way exist and cast their shadows before them, especially if they are disasters of some magnitude, so that certain people receive premonitions of such disasters, does it make sense to set up a bureau to which such people could send accounts of their premonitions? Such bureaus have indeed been created, the British one being set up in January 1967 after the Aberfan disaster the year before. Mr Andrew Mackenzie has studied the British bureau's cases. In his book *The riddle of the future*, he describes a number of the cases that suggest that somehow information about future events can be obtained – in which case it is difficult to avoid the conclusion that in some way the future is 'there' already. If this is so, what are the implications for the existence of free will?

Blotting his copybook

The prophecies of Nostradamus (right) have been famous for more than four centuries. Written in *quatrains*, or four-line verses, they are extremely difficult to understand. Certain interpretations have, however, become standard: among the claims made for Nostradamus's verses are that they predict the French Revolution and the accession of an emperor called Napoloron – and, perhaps the most famous of the alleged prophecies, that they forecast the rise of Hister, or Hitler.

A closer look at these enigmatic verses, however, shows them to be far less ambitious examples of prophecy. The reference to the retirement of a great personage to a small place is not a description of Napoleon's exile on Elba, but of the retirement of the emperor Charles v, an event that had taken place shortly *before* the publication of the 'prophecy'. Nostradamus's references to 'Bretaigne' are to Brittany, not Britain – thus predictions of political unrest in 'Bretaigne' do not refer to turbulent periods in Britain's history. And, it turns out, 'Hister' is not a near-miss for 'Hitler' – but means the river Danube.

The three ages of Man, by Lorenzo Lotto (1480–1556). Some psychical researchers have suggested that the entire course of our lives is subconsciously known to us – that, in some way, our past and future are always present

Living in the past

Timeslips into the past seem to indicate that the past really is always with us – and that it exists on a level that is accessible to psychics. The implications of this fascinating idea are enormous

THERE IS A SURPRISINGLY large body of evidence to support the view that, on certain occasions, direct access to the past is possible. The term *retrocognition* is often used to describe events in which a person experiences a past scene. This scene may have happened recently, or many centuries in the past. Sight and sound may be involved either separately or together.

It comes as a surprise to many to discover that it is at least as difficult to provide a cast-iron case for retrocognition as it is for precognition. The difficulty arises when a case of alleged retrocognition is reported and a serious attempt is made to ensure that the person who apparently viewed a past scene actually did so, and did not draw upon records such as history books, newspapers, documents, descriptions by other people, memories and so on. The person may be sincere in his assertion that he had had no prior experience of the scene. But memory is fallible. It is safe to say that many of the events of our past life have created memories that have receded into the unconscious and cannot be recaptured at will. If the hallucination mechanism that is a part of our mental make-up draws upon such memories and, for some reason, reconstructs the relevant scene, it is certainly possible that we may not realise we are actually dramatising our own experiences rather than having a genuine retrocognition.

The possibility of viewing the past obviously carries the implication that, in some way, the past is still in existence and accessible. But, however difficult that idea may be, it does not raise the difficulties caused by the idea of premonitions. There, the uncomfortable corresponding suggestion that in some way the *future* is already in existence and accessible produces painful paradoxes.

It is surely safe to say that, whereas it is not impossible to visualise the existence of a machine for viewing the past, it appears to be conceptually impossible to visualise a machine for viewing the future. Common sense tells us that the past is over and done with and cannot be changed even if observed anew; on the other hand the future is yet to be and, if we do not like what we think may happen, we are free to change it by an act of will – or, if not, then surely there is no free will.

Let us consider some of the many alleged cases of retrocognition. In his pioneering work *Human personality and its survival of bodily death*, Frederic Myers described the crystal-gazing visions of a young lady known as Miss A. She was closely associated with the Countess of Radnor, who verified a number of her alleged visions of past scenes. She was also well-known to Myers.

Describing a retrocognitive scene viewed in the crystal while she was staying at Lord and Lady Radnor's home, Longford Castle, near Salisbury, Wiltshire, Miss A. said:

Lady Radnor was in the room with me. I saw amongst other things a large carved fireplace with a coat of arms in the middle and curious serpents' heads. I seemed to follow this path which seemed to lead out by a river and I saw figures pass along it in old-fashioned dress. The name Edwye de Bovery was then spelt out in the crystal; and Lady Radnor said that the vision must be all wrong, as the name had never been spelt like that. The name 'White Webs' was also spelt out – a name of which I had never heard. A few days afterwards, when I was looking at some books in the library, I saw a curious old book with crests and coats of arms, drawn by hand, not printed; and in this book I found one of the coats of arms which I had seen in the crystal . . . . Lady Radnor found that it was the coat belonging to an heiress Miss Smith. A little while afterwards, in an old church register or account book or something, the name of Sir Edwye de Bovery was found.

In attesting to this, Lady Radnor reported that it was in the local church register.

Sir Edward des Bouverie, Kt., whose name I have since found spelt in old deeds de Bovery, though he signed it himself des Bouverie, lived at the Red House, Cheshunt, Herts., and died there in 1694. His son, Sir William, sold the house and lived partly at the parsonage of Cheshunt. There is a place called White Webs in that neighbourhood. Sir Edward's grandson, Edward des Bouverie, sold the property and settled at Longford in 1717. In 1718 he married Mary Smith, daughter and co-heiress of John Smith of London, one of the first Governors of the Bank of England. There were many secret passages leading to and from the Red House at Cheshunt; but I have not tried to identify the house at White Webs.

On another occasion, Miss A. had a vision in Salisbury Cathedral. She saw vast processions of gorgeously apparelled Catholic ecclesiastics with jewelled crosses carried before them. Among the dignitaries was one who came near them and gazed at them with a singularly sad expression. He said, 'I have been a great sinner. I was greatly responsible for the beheading of Anne Boleyn. What adds to the sadness of it, her father and I were boys together, and our homes were in close proximity to each other.' On being asked his name, he said: 'My name is John Longland.' On being further questioned he replied: 'Mr Barnby's music brought me here. I often hear it in Eton Chapel.'

Investigation showed that John Longland had been Dean of Salisbury in Henry VIII's reign, also that his body had been buried in Eton College chapel. This fact was not known locally because the brass that covered the tomb had been destroyed by vandals in the 17th century. Mr Barnby, whose 'music brought me here', was Sir Joseph Barnby,

Right: Lady Radnor (1820–1879) and her home, Longford Castle, near Salisbury, Wiltshire (below). It was at Longford that a certain Miss A., gazing into a crystal ball, experienced a retrocognitive vision of the house as it had been around the end of the 17th century. Astonishingly, the vision included details that were unknown to both Miss A. and the Countess, and were verified only afterwards

the well-known Victorian musician.

If we accept Miss A.'s claim that she was describing accurately the visions she saw, we have some curious facts to explain. It seems impossible to dismiss them or the other remarkable visions of the past she experienced over the years. On the one hand, it would appear that she was directly viewing people and buildings as they had been, in some cases centuries before; on the other hand the 'people' she saw actually seemed to converse with her and in some cases claimed to be still around and interested in contemporary events, for example Sir Joseph Barnby's music. It is cases like these that defy a simple clear-cut explanation, either of retrocognition of a 'dead' past or of survival.

A musical phantasm

In an incident from the United States, researchers Gardner Murphy and Herbert L. Klemme reported a case of alleged retrocognition involving Mrs Coleen Buterbaugh, a secretary at Nebraska Wesleyan University, Lincoln, USA. Mrs Buterbaugh's experience occurred on 3 October 1963 when she was asked by Dean Sam Dahl to take a message to a colleague, Professor Martin, in his office suite in the C.C. White Building nearby. As she entered the building and walked through its large hall, she heard the sounds of students in some rooms reserved for music practice. In particular, she heard the sound of a marimba being played. Entering the first room of the suite, she halted after a few steps when she experienced a strong smell – a musty, unpleasant odour. She had been walking with her eyes downcast, but now she raised them – and saw the figure of a very tall, black-haired woman in a shirt-waisted, ankle-length skirt reaching with her right arm towards the upper right-hand shelves in an old music cabinet.

Mrs Buterbaugh later described her experiences in these words:

> As I first walked into the room everything was quite normal. About four steps into the room was when the strong odor hit me. When I say strong odor, I mean the kind that simply stops you in your tracks and almost chokes you. I was looking down at the floor, as one often does when walking, and as soon as that odor stopped me I felt that there was someone in the room with me. It was then that I was aware that there were no noises out in the hall. Everything was deathly quiet. I looked up and something drew my eyes to the cabinet along the wall in the next room. I looked up and there she was. She had her back to me, reaching up into one of the shelves of the cabinet with her right hand, and standing perfectly still. She never moved. She was not transparent, and yet I knew she wasn't real. While I was looking at her she just faded away – not parts of her body one at a time, but her whole body all at once.

> Up until the time she faded away I was not aware of anyone else being in the suite of rooms, but just about the time of her fading out I felt as though I still was not alone. To my left was a desk and I had a feeling there was a man sitting at that desk. I turned around and saw no one, but I still felt his presence. When that feeling of his presence left I have no idea, because it was then, when I looked out the window behind that desk, that I got frightened and left the room . . . when I looked out that window there wasn't one modern thing out there. The street [Madison Street], which is less than a half block away from the building, was not even there and neither was the new Willard House. That was when I realised that these people were not in my time, but that I was back in their time.

> It was not until I was back out in the

Above: the C.C. White building of Nebraska Wesleyan University, Lincoln, USA. It was here on 3 October 1963 that Mrs Coleen Buterbaugh had a spontaneous and extraordinarily vivid retrocognitive vision: walking into the music office (above right), she saw the figure of a tall woman in a long skirt and bouffant hairstyle. Research later revealed that a Miss Clarissa U. Mills, who fitted Mrs Buterbaugh's description of her vision, had died in the office in 1936

> hall that I again heard the familiar noises. This must have all taken place in a few seconds because the girls that were going into the orientation class as I entered the room were still going in and someone was still playing the marimba.

Shaken by her experience, Mrs Buterbaugh returned to her office. She tried to continue typing, but kept stopping. Finally she told Dean Dahl of the strange event. In later discussions, it was suggested that there could have been some resemblance between the tall black-haired woman Mrs Buterbaugh had seen in the office and a Miss Clarissa U. Mills, a lecturer in musical theory and piano, who had used that office many years before and who had died suddenly in 1936 in a room just across the hall. In some old yearbooks (never before seen by Mrs Buterbaugh), a picture of Miss Mills was found. The figure had been standing with its back towards Mrs Buterbaugh so that the face was hidden, but in many particulars it resembled Miss Mills, who had been very tall, thin and black-haired. She had been interested in music and choral singing – and the filing cabinet before which the apparition had stood actually contained choral music, some of which dated back to a time before Miss Mills's death. In addition, the clothes and bushy, bouffant hairstyle of the apparition were consistent with the fashions of 1915. Miss Mills had started work at the college in 1912, and in the picture of her discovered in an old yearbook she wore just such a hairstyle.

Mrs Buterbaugh was able to describe what she saw when she looked out of the window behind the desk.

The window was open. Even though it was fairly early in the morning, it

Right: Gardner Murphy, American psychologist and psychical researcher who, with Herbert L. Klemme, made a detailed study of Mrs Coleen Buterbaugh's experience at Nebraska Wesleyan University

appeared as though it were a very warm, summer afternoon. It was very still. There were a few scattered trees – about two on my right and about three on my left. It seems to me there were more, but these are the only ones I can be definite about. The rest was open field; the new Willard sorority house and also Madison Street were not there. I remember seeing a very vague outline of some sort of building to my right and that is about all. Nothing else but open field.

Of interest is the fact that the Professor Martin to whom Mrs Buterbaugh had been told to take a message was a visiting music professor from Scotland, and at that time he was busy arranging choral group singing –

something Miss Mills must often have done.

Miss Mills died in the office across the hall one day shortly before 9 a.m., having struggled through a bitter wind to the C.C. White Building. Mrs Buterbaugh also arrived there shortly before 9 a.m.

There are obvious resemblances between the cases described here. The most famous, if controversial, is surely the seeming visitation in 1901 by Miss Moberley and Miss Jourdain to the grounds of the Palace of Versailles at the time of Marie-Antoinette.

In *Human personality* Frederic Myers, discussing phantoms of the dead, wondered if the influence of certain houses in generating apparitions should be included under the broader heading of retrocognition.

Manifestations which occur in haunted houses depend, let us say, on something which has taken place a long time ago. In what way do they depend on that past event? Are they a sequel or only a residue? Is there fresh operation going on, or only fresh perception of something already accomplished? Or can we in such a case draw any real distinction between a continued perception of a past action?

The passage quoted highlights a main problem of alleged hauntings. In modern terms, are they psychic tape recordings, available to be played by a human psychic 'tape recorder' brought to the scene, or is the percipient directly 'viewing' the past event or events, or is there evidence of purpose, of a desire from an entity 'on the other side' – to put it vaguely – to deal with unfinished business? The possibility that the past is still 'there' and at times accessible must evidently be seriously considered in any attempt to understand the nature of time.

Time: the last frontier

Left: a Brazilian Spiritist in trance. Some psychical researchers have suggested that the subconscious mind has access to information about the future – and that, in certain circumstances, for instance when the mind is in a trance, this information can cross the barrier between the unconscious and conscious minds in the form of a premonition

Below: Hermann Minkowski (1864–1909), the German physicist who first suggested that the Universe can be described in terms of four-dimensional space-time

Psychics appear to be able to move backwards and forwards in time, at will or spontaneously. How does this fit in with the scientists' idea of a Universe in which time has no direction?

DO PRECOGNITIONS and retrocognitions exist and, if so, do they provide important clues to the nature of time? Many well-known philosophers and psychologists have taken seriously the evidence for precognitions and retrocognitions and have accepted that our 'common-sense' ideas of time may be false and misleading, in the same way as the theoretical physicists of the late 19th century came to realise that their ideas about space and time were wrong, especially in the subatomic and astronomical realms. By 1908 Hermann Minkowski was suggesting that the Universe could be described in terms of four-dimensional space-time. In fact, he was introducing what has now come to be called the block Universe, a static universe with no past, present or future except that introduced by the observer (see page 80). The observer's consciousness travels along his world line through the block Universe like a spotlight moving over a dark landscape or field. Those bits of the field the spotlight has already picked out, the observer terms the past; those that are yet to appear in the spotlight he terms the future.

William James, the American psychologist, introduced the concept of the 'specious present', a small but finite chunk of space-time containing everything that the observer is consciously perceiving at that moment.

The psychical researcher H.F. Saltmarsh modified this theory in an attempt to account for precognition and retrocognition. He supposed that the conscious mind's specious present was smaller than the subconscious's specious present. Thus, Saltmarsh argued, it is perfectly possible that an event that lies in the 'future' of the conscious mind may lie in the specious present of the subconscious. If this event were unpleasant or likely to be dangerous to the person concerned, the subconscious might warn the conscious mind by presenting it with a premonition in the form of a dream. If the conditions are right, the premonition may even appear as a vision while the person is wide awake. Premonitory dreams are, however, commoner – and many premonitions are received in a generally relaxed and receptive state of mind while the subject is either emerging from or approaching sleep, or in a comfortable chair reading a book or watching television.

Saltmarsh did not, however, like the implications of his theory for the question of free will. If the future is simply a collection of events that make up the static block Universe, and if the events that make up a person's life are simply strung out in a line within the block Universe to be approached in a set order, then it seems there can be no free will. Saltmarsh modified his theory in the light of this objection by assuming that the future is in some way plastic and modifiable, and it is only when an event is experienced or becomes a past event that it becomes 'set' so that it cannot thereafter be modified.

It is possible, however, to construct a theory that goes some way towards accounting for the fact that, even if a premonition of a future event has taken place, this does not necessarily mean that the event itself is inevitable.

Let us suppose that the spotlight on the block Universe that contains everything consciously perceived by the person at that moment is surrounded by a hazy ring that represents the subconscious. Within this are all the events being perceived by the person's subconscious.

Let us take a concrete example. Let the world line be that of a girl who is scheduled to sail on the *Titanic* in April 1912. She buys her ticket, packs her bags and has them loaded into the hold of the great liner, and is about to embark. But at that instant the event of the liner's sinking is illuminated by the ring of her subconscious, although it still lies

The American psychologist William James (1842–1910), who invented the concept of the 'specious present' – a small chunk of space-time containing everything perceived by the observer at a given instant

outside the spotlight of her conscious. The sinking is therefore still in her future, in common-sense terms. But somehow a symbolic representation of the terrible scenes perceived by her subconscious manages to cross the threshold between subconscious and conscious, and she experiences a premonition of her own death. So she changes her mind about sailing, thus changing her world line across the dark field of the Universe so that she avoids dying on the liner. And, some days in the future, she reads about the liner sinking and no doubt congratulates herself on her premonition for saving her life.

The point to note is that the two events – the death of the girl in the *Titanic* disaster, and her change of mind and survival – are equally real in a potential sense, in that they are both events in the dark field of the Universe; the only difference between them is that the girl's conscious spotlight illuminated one, and not the other.

A further consequence of this theory is that, since the dark field of the Universe contains all possible events and presumably therefore all world lines, both branches of the girl's world line must exist, so we must assume that there are many, many branches and junction points; the decision taken at any moment decides which branch of the tree of world lines the conscious and unconscious spotlight will travel along. This is reminiscent of the theoretical physicist Hugh Everett's concept of a multiply branching universe in which every probability is realised but only one branch is observed. The

Right: the *Titanic* leaves port on her maiden voyage. Like many other disasters, the sinking of the *Titanic* was the subject of a large number of premonitions. Some scientists believe that subconscious knowledge of future catastrophes is forced to become conscious through the distress it causes the subconscious mind

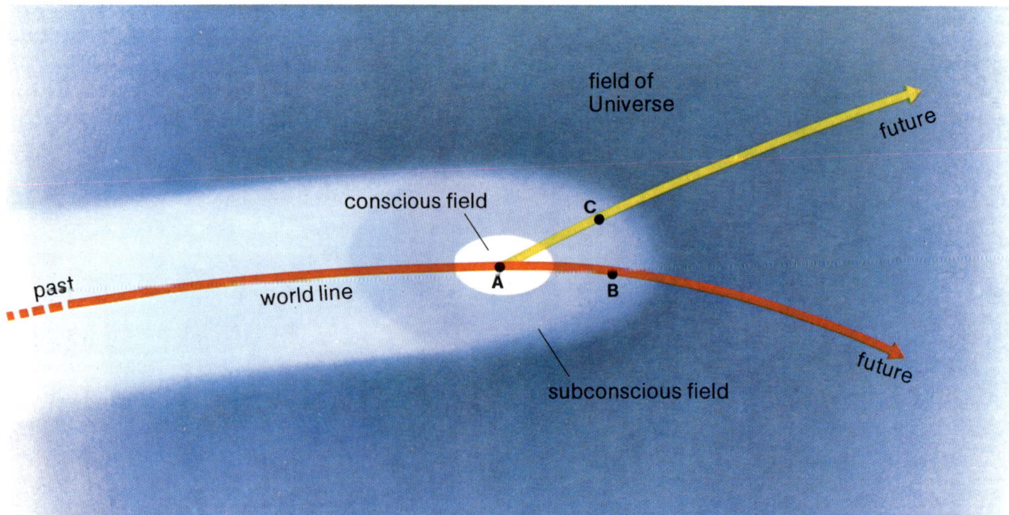

experiences that make up a person's life, on this theory, are rather like those of a man who enters an art gallery at night, his only illumination being a spotlight that he trains on the pictures of the corridor along which he is travelling. He sees scenes of his early childhood and boyhood, and then he comes in the darkness to a 'T' junction. He can go either left or right. He chooses to go left and continues to shine his torch on the pictures on the wall of the left-hand corridor. He sees himself in these pictures as a youth carrying out various actions, going to various places, making various friends, until he becomes a man. He never sees the pictures of what his life would have been had he made a decision that took him right instead of left. He does not see, for example, that he would have died in a car accident at the age of 23. Instead he sees himself finished with university studies, taking a good job, marrying and having children.

There are other interesting implications about this theory of time and the Universe. A human being may be looked upon as the sum of a conscious field, subconscious field and a body. The body is embedded in the block Universe. What we call our body is only an instantaneous slice of a larger and longer entity, the 'body envelope' – the world line the spotlight of consciousness travels along. It seems reasonable to regard a person, alive and in a state of consciousness, as equivalent to conscious field plus subconscious field plus body envelope. If so, is an unconscious or dreaming person equivalent to subconscious field plus body envelope?

Spiritual paths

It may be that a psychic's subconscious field has the freedom to wander over the dark field of the Universe, probing until it intersects the world path of another person. In this case perhaps subconscious field plus body envelope equals unconscious or dreaming person – or perhaps at least in some cases the alleged spirit who communicates through a psychic. And there is also the intriguing possibility that if two subconscious fields, but not the corresponding conscious fields,

Above: an observer's consciousness travelling through space-time can be represented by spotlight A moving across a dark field. Around the bright spot is a hazy ring of light that represents the observer's subconscious. On this theory, it is possible for a catastrophe B to enter the observer's subconscious field and appear as a premonition that causes the observer to alter his world line to pass through an event C to avoid it. It is also possible to explain the telepathic activity of psychics such as Eileen Garrett (below left): perhaps conditions for telepathy exist when the subconscious fields, but not the conscious fields, of the subjects overlap (below)

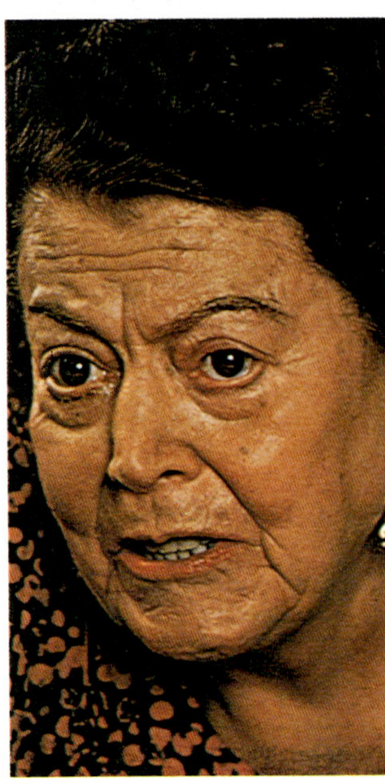

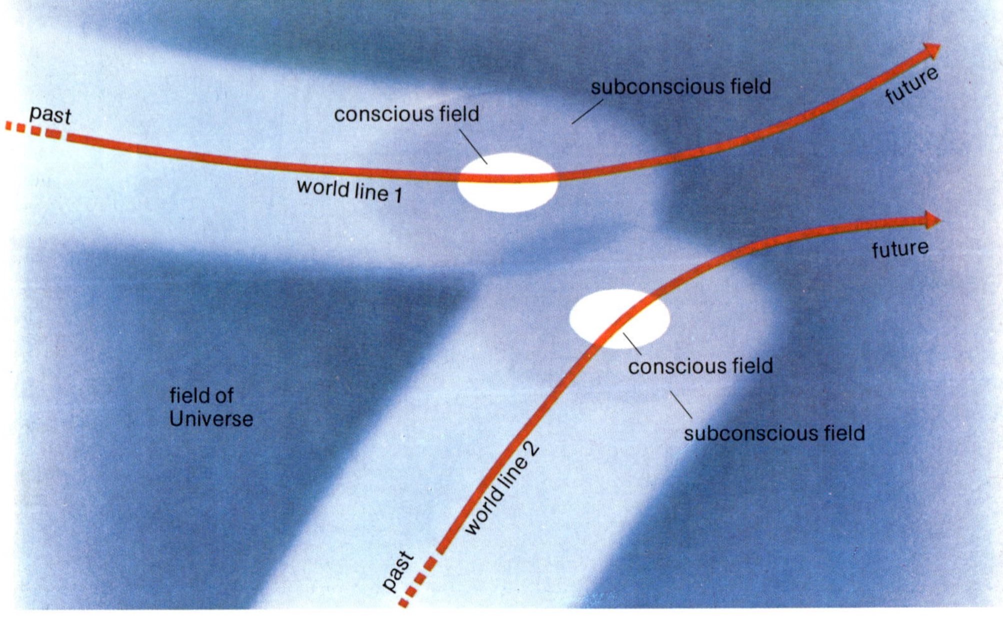

intersect then the right conditions for telepathic communication are created.

It has been suggested by a number of psychologists and psychical researchers that perhaps the ring of unconscious perception covers the whole lifespan of a human being. For example, Aniela Jaffé has suggested that, at his deepest level, a human being has knowledge of his whole life, and Professor Tenhaeff has remarked that the psychic may derive his paranormal knowledge of his sitter through telepathy from the sitter's psyche. The philosopher Henri Bergson speculated that one of the tasks of the brain may be to restrict this view of time to a particular moment – as in J.W. Dunne's theory of time (see page 66), in which the consciousness of the human being is confined to the present moment, but a higher self in sleep is allowed views of past and future events in his life. The American parapsychologist Lawrence LeShan has pointed to the opinions of many mystics and psychics that, in their altered states of consciousness, time and space are irrelevant, there is no yesterday, today or tomorrow, and no passing of time. As the medium Eileen Garrett said, 'In the ultimate nature of the Universe there are no divisions in time and space' – a view that is not fundamentally in disagreement with the teachings of modern quantum mechanics.

It really looks, in fact, as if our consciousness *creates* time so that it is an illusion – a view that is in accordance with Eastern mystical teaching. Future study of precognitions and retrocognitions will possibly be able to define more clearly the problems bound up with the study of the nature of time – for example, the problem of free will and precognition, the idea that cause always precedes effect, the possibility that, given a precognition, the future can be changed by action taken on the part of the percipient, and so on. Philosophers C.D. Broad, C.W.K. Mundle, H.H. Price and many others have already turned their minds to these problems. The fact that such people are prepared to utilise the evidence for precognition and retrocognition in tackling the question of the nature of time shows that the subject is recognised as one of the most important research fields of science.

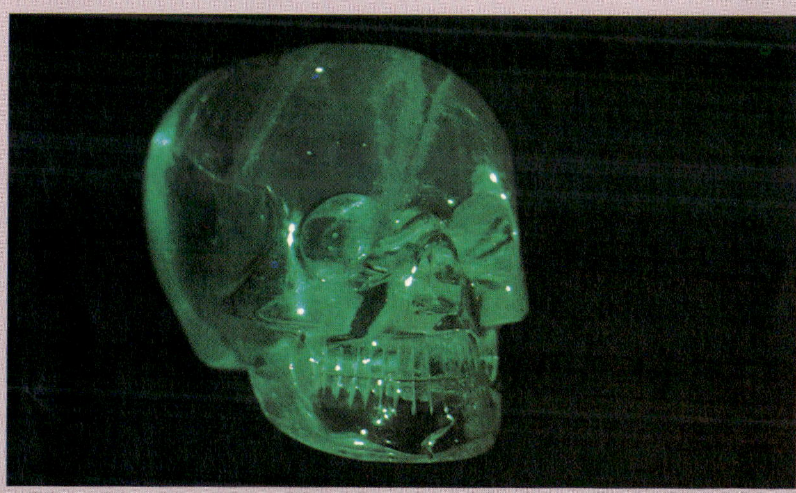

Picking and choosing

How is it that psychics appear to have private access to information about the past and the future? One suggestion is that they are simply using a secret information retrieval system.

Librarians are well aware of the fact that the disorder of a system is often only apparent. The traditional way of storing books by subject and author's name alphabetically is not the only way. Books may be put anywhere, the shelves being filled in an apparently random way as long as an unambiguous information storage and retrieval system is used.

For example, a book on the Milky Way will be physically located on the library shelves devoted to astronomy and lie between Barr and Bartlett because the author's name is Barrett. In the library's storage and retrieval systems, however, it may be located with three other books by Krupp, Nash and Lawrence because all three books are about the Milky Way. If the library's retrieval system is triggered with the request for books on the subject 'Milky Way', all four books will appear – even though Lawrence's book is devoted to the well-known confection called 'Milky Way'! If one did not know that an information retrieval system was operating, one might be tempted to think that the appearance of Lawrence's book with the astronomical ones was a meaningful gastronomic synchronicity – or to dismiss it as a coincidence.

In a similar way, a hologram viewed with the naked eye does not form any recognisable image, but when illuminated by a laser beam, it produces an astonishing three-dimensional one (left).

Assuming that the seeming disorder of life *does* make sense when the correct retrieval system is applied, it is possible to see time as merely an illusion produced by our pedestrian consciousnesses as they traverse the block Universe. The tricks of time – precognitions, timeslips, the ability of psychics to scan at will the long-gone past or the as yet unrealised future – are freak effects of an information storage and retrieval system. If this hypothesis is true, certain questions become relevant: What are the rules for retrieving information from the system? Can anyone learn them? And even, is it meaningful to ask who or what is responsible for the system? And perhaps if it has a physical existence, it can be located. But where?

Most of us believe that time flows along steadily 'like an ever-rolling stream'. But modern science is discovering that the reality may be far more complex – and that time travel may be physically possible. JOHN GRIBBIN reports

WE ARE ALL TIME TRAVELLERS, moving a certain distance in time with every full rotation of the Earth – a distance that is generally shared by everyone else. That is the reality of our everyday lives – but who has not speculated on the possibility of varying this steady progress, so that we either speed up while everything around us seems to move more slowly, or somehow drag our feet so that everything hurries by while we are left behind? And what of the possibility of travel backwards down that same road, to visit the past and even, perhaps, to alter it? Even if physical time travel is impossible, or impracticable, what about the possibility of communication across time, in the form of dreams, visions and ghosts from the past?

Surprisingly, perhaps, science does acknowledge the possibility of physical time travel, in certain circumstances. This, however, demands a new way of looking at reality. To provide a bridge between our everyday experience of time rolling steadily forward and the bizarre possibilities that stem from abandoning this common-sense view, it is best to look first at some of the puzzles and paradoxes inherent in the possibility of time travel. The discovery of a paradox, to the unimaginative, demonstrates

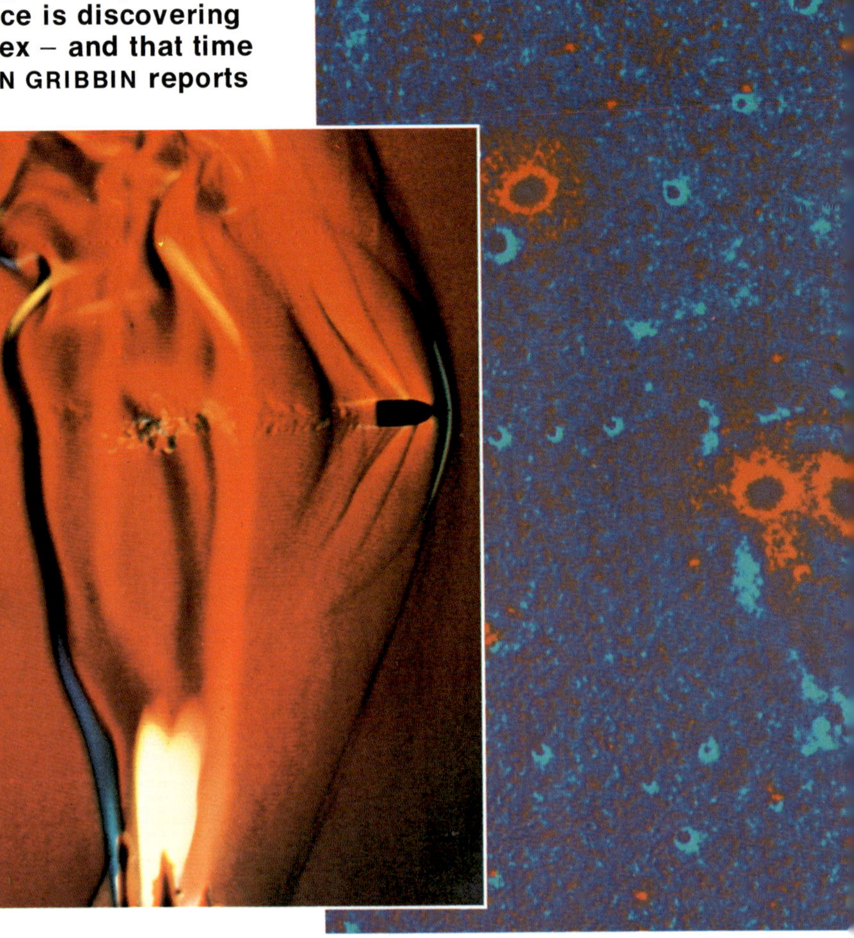

From time to time

Science is based on the notion of causality: that events follow their causes – a bullet leaves the gun *after* you pull the trigger, not before. But what if, seeing the bullet in flight (above), you were able to travel back in time and prevent the trigger being pulled? Such problems have led some scientists to reject the possibility of time travel. Yet one day the invention of a working time machine may provide as forceful a refutation of their view as this space photograph of the Earth (left) does of the idea, held by most medieval scholars until the 13th century, that the Earth was flat

that time travel is impossible. To the truly imaginative, however, a paradox is a challenge to find a more radical solution.

Scientists have had to become accustomed to doing without common sense. The idea of a steady flow of time is already outmoded by experiments involving particles that travel at speeds close to the speed of light, under conditions where Einstein's theory of relativity, far removed from the usual world of common sense, provides the best description of how the Universe works. Time, like space, is elastic, not rigid, and Einstein's description involves a blending together in which time and space are seen as two sides of the same coin, a coin dubbed 'space-time'. In this concept, both time and space can be stretched and squeezed, depending on circumstances, and time can be traded for space as long as the appropriate total balance is maintained. This is all solid, sober scientific fact.

Relativity theory is confirmed by the direct measurement of what happens to subatomic particles whirled at huge speeds inside modern 'atom-smasher' machines – accelerators. It is fact, not speculation, that such a

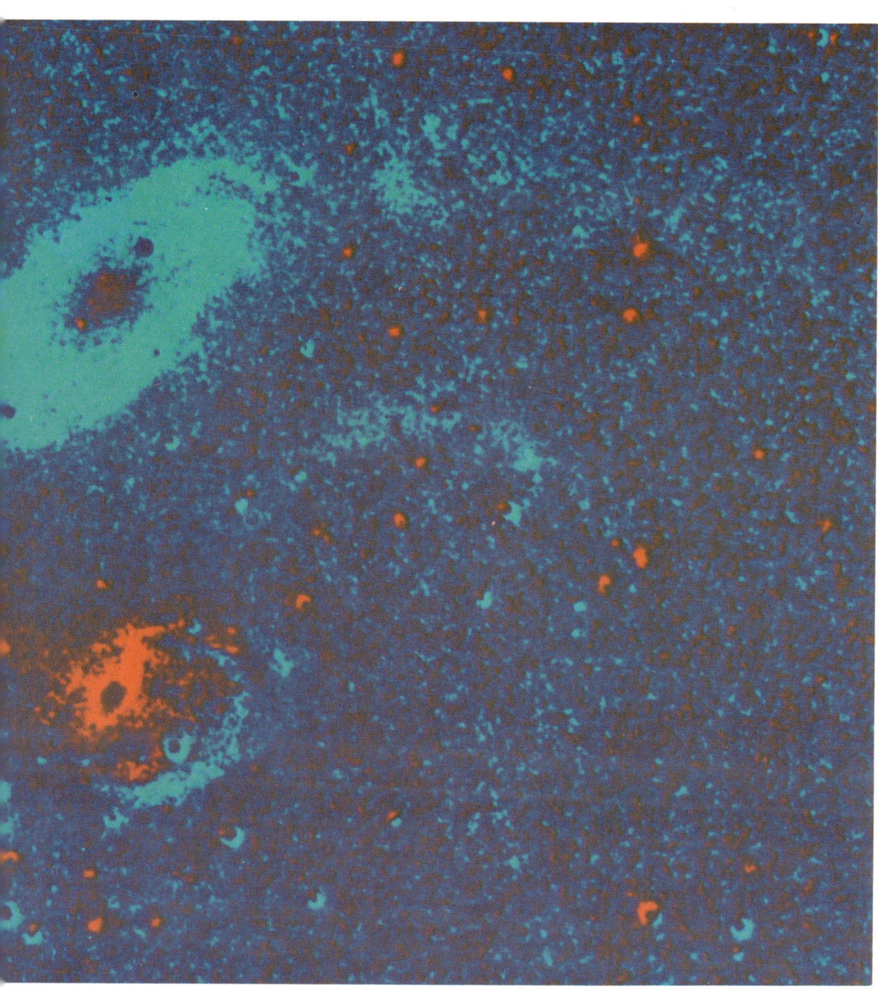

always follow their causes, in an orderly procession. A bullet leaves the gun *after* the trigger is pulled, not before; the results of the 3.15 at Ascot reach us only *after* the race is run, not in time for us to be able to rush round to the betting shop and make a killing. The logical implication is that if time travel involves violation of causality, then it must be impossible. If a theory tells us we can commit suicide, *then* go to a restaurant and enjoy a good dinner then, the argument goes, there must be something wrong with the theory. This is not a scientific proof or disproof. It is a matter of philosophy and logical argument – and the Universe may yet hold a few surprises for logicians.

But the science-fiction philosophers have their own answers to these paradoxes, and their version of the debate highlights two possibilities – branches and loops in time. The hoariest example of a time travel paradox, science fiction or philosophy, concerns a traveller who goes back in time and, wittingly or unwittingly, prevents the birth of the person who would have been his grandfather. If so, he could never have been born himself; so it must be the case that the grandfather *was* born, after all; so it *was* possible for our hero to go back in time to prevent the birth of his ancestor . . . and so on. The existence of the paradox is seen by many people as proof that time travel is impossible. Just as nature was once said to 'abhor a vacuum', now we might say that she 'abhors time travel'. But it is very easy to

Above: an image-processed photograph of the Stephan's Quintet group of galaxies. Scientists believe that time becomes distorted near large, dense masses – such as stars or black holes – making time travel possible

Right: a Van de Graaff electrostatic accelerator at the Atomic Energy Research Establishment at Harwell, Oxfordshire, England, used to speed subatomic particles to high velocities. Experiment has shown that such particles have longer lives than their stationary counterparts – so that, for them, time passes more slowly

particle has a longer lifetime than a stationary counterpart; and it is fact that an astronaut sent on a journey at a speed that is a sizeable fraction of the speed of light – 186,000 miles per second (300,000 kilometres per second) – ages less than the rest of us left behind on Earth.

Another way to stretch time, entirely within accepted modern scientific thinking, involves sitting in a strong gravitational field – the sort of gravitational field you might get near a sizeable black hole. This does not necessitate travelling through the black hole, just sitting in its gravitational field and watching the Universe go by, seemingly at a speeded-up rate. Both tricks are forms of time travel – they get the intrepid astronaut into the future 'faster' than the usual rate. But if he doesn't like what he finds there, there is no way home. Time may not be a *steadily* flowing stream, but even within the framework of modern science it is usually regarded as a one-way street. Hurrying forward may, just, be possible; bucking the stream and swimming back into the past just isn't on. The reason why such possibilities are dismissed lies in the existence of certain paradoxes. And the best way to get some idea of the paradoxes and possibilities is to look in the pages of science fiction.

The key to the discussion is causality – the seemingly logical assumption that events

Above: Christ's triumphal entry into Jerusalem. In his novel *Behold the man*, Michael Moorcock describes a fanatical Christian who journeys back to the time of Christ. He sees no sign of the Jesus described in the gospels. As he tries to tell people the gospel story, he finds himself playing out the role of Christ – thus making it possible, 2000 years later, for a religious fanatic to become inspired by the story and, travelling back in time, to re-enact a story he himself has created

Right: one philosophical theory of time sees all possible combinations of events as somehow running parallel to our own. Thus everything that can possibly be imagined to happen *does* happen – somewhere along the infinite array of parallel worlds. Some of these may differ from our normal, everyday existence only by a single detail; others may be quite fantastic. It has been suggested by some theorists that both dreams and paranormal events – such as this psychic warning of a mining disaster to Andrew Jackson Davis (far right) – could be 'leaks' of information from parallel worlds into our own

imagine resolutions to this simple paradox in which the grandfather is both born and not born, the grandson both exists and does not exist. The simplest answer is that the effects of the time traveller's activities are already rooted in the fabric of time and space – his visit to the past cannot change the present because that visit is already part of history.

Michael Moorcock developed the theme in his novel *Behold the man*. In this, the time traveller is a disturbed individual with a tendency to religious mania, who journeys back to the time of Jesus to view the crucifixion. His time machine is destroyed beyond repair, and he finds no trace of the Jesus described in the Bible. Inexorably, as he attempts to tell people about the Jesus he came to see, he is drawn into the rôle of Jesus, playing out the events he remembers from the Bible, up to and including the crucifixion. So history is created, and the Bible stories are written down, ensuring that in 2000 years time a certain individual will travel back in time to close the loop, like the snake that eats its own tail.

This resolution of the paradox sees time as fixed in some greater fabric, with ourselves almost literally merely actors playing out predetermined roles on the stage of space-time. The alternative resolution of the paradox sees space-time as infinitely variable, with each of us master of his or her own destiny to an extent few people ever dream of. Again, an example from science fiction makes the point. In *Lest darkness fall*, L. Sprague de Camp's hero is a 20th-century man who is mysteriously deposited in sixth-century Italy and averts the Dark Ages single-handed. The story is hokum; but the author's explanation is that, having 'slipped down the trunk' of the tree of history, the hero has created a new branch, a new line of history growing out as a result of his introduction of 20th-century ideas into a sixth-century environment. With only slight modifications, this idea becomes the respectable philosophical concept of parallel universes, worlds running alongside one another in some sense, with an infinite number of variations on the theme of history. If you go back and kill your grandfather, the argument runs, you have also slipped 'sideways' into a parallel reality where the grandfather always was killed by an intruder

from elsewhere (and elsewhen). So when you come home to find history unchanged, don't be surprised – in your timeline, nothing has happened to change history at all!

Taken to its logical conclusion, this view of reality argues that we have complete control over our destiny, because literally anything is possible, and happens somewhere among the infinite array of parallel universes. All we have to do is find a way to travel across the time barrier, not forwards or backwards but *sideways* in time. It is, of course, much easier said than done; but if physical time travel remains at the very least an unlikely prospect for us, there remains the intriguing possibility that dreams, ghosts and other phenomena classified as paranormal experiences could be just as well – perhaps better – explained in terms of information somehow leaking into our world from parallel worlds of time as by direct communication, involving time travel, from the future or past of our own timeline.

An absurd illusion

One of the most startling philosophical theories sees *everything* as being in the mind. Sir Fred Hoyle, an eminent astronomer who has a penchant for speculation and science fiction, mentioned this idea in a serious scientific book, *Ten faces of the Universe*, and elaborated on the theme in his science-fiction novel *October the first is too late*. 'Time like an ever-rolling stream bears all his sons away' – the image of time conveyed by the famous words of the ninetieth psalm – is 'a grotesque and absurd illusion'. In fact, all the events that we imagine making up the flow of time – as well as all other imaginable events – exist in a kind of infinite sorting office, with each

event, or state, in its own pigeon hole. Hoyle goes on:

Suppose that in each of these states your own consciousness is included. As soon as a particular state is chosen, as soon as an imaginary office worker takes a look at the contents of a particular pigeon hole, you have the subjective consciousness of a particular moment, of what you call the present. Think of the clerk in an office taking a look, first at the contents of one pigeon hole, then at the contents of another. Suppose he does this, not in sequence,

Above: Rod Taylor stars in the 1960 MGM film *The time machine*, based on the novel by H. G. Wells. Such stories raise an exciting question: could it be that mankind will one day be capable of building a working time machine?

but in any old order. What is the effect on your subjective consciousness? So far as the clerk himself is concerned, he's jumping about all over the place among the pigeon holes. So your consciousness jumps all over the place. But the strange thing is that your subjective impression is quite different. You have the impression of time as an ever-rolling stream.

We may all, in fact, be experiencing time travel, as well as travel between different possible universes – but, because one of the rules of the game is that the clerk in the office can look at only one pigeon hole at a time, we never know it.

True or not, theories such as these show that there is more to time than we may suppose – and that there are, philosophically speaking, ways round the paradoxes of time travel. And if there are ways round the paradoxes, there is no logical reason why it should not be possible one day to build a physical time machine.

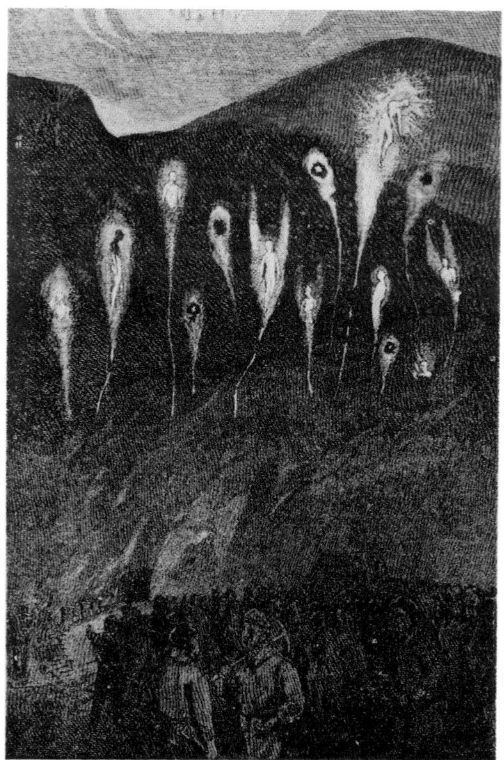

Blueprint for a time machine

If time travel is possible in principle, how can it be achieved? Super-dense neutron stars could be the means by which, one day, space travellers will be able to journey into the past

THE PHILOSOPHICAL DEBATE about the paradoxes of time travel makes one thing clear: it is possible to imagine ways in which the Universe may be constructed so that time travel, of some kind or another, may be allowed by the laws of physics. That leaves the big question: is time travel *really* possible? And, if so, how could a time machine be built?

During the 1970s, there was a great deal of excitement about the implications of the existence of black holes for time travel. A black hole is a region of space in which enough matter is concentrated for gravity to make a 'hole' in space-time, a region from which no energy – light energy included – can possibly escape. The idea of such black holes as holes in space is an entirely re-spectable part of modern astrophysics, and they are invoked by scientists to explain a number of strange phenomena. Energy re-leased from black holes could, for instance, explain the genesis of high-energy x-rays that have been observed in our own Galaxy and, on a much grander scale, the energy sources that appear to lie at the centres of certain galaxies. A black hole is a hole in space – but, as Einstein taught us, space and time are inseparable, two facets of space-time. It seems reasonable to suppose that a hole in space must also be a hole in time,

Above: a nearby artificial satellite draws a streak of light across the background of thousands of distant stars revealed by a long-exposure photograph. Many astronomers believe that, in the immensity of our Galaxy, there are numerous black holes. Will they one day be harnessed for time travel?

whatever that means – and if it were possible to travel 'through' a black hole, we might emerge in some other place, perhaps even another universe, and at some other time. Unfortunately, however, such speculation seems to be nothing more than science fic-tion, because the journey through the black hole would crush you to death and rip you apart simultaneously. But nevertheless, the discovery of black holes has set a whole new generation of theorists thinking about the possibility of time travel.

According to modern theories of space-time – refinements of Einstein's theory of general relativity – the key to time travel is not black holes, but what are called naked singularities. A singularity is a place where the laws of physics as we know them break down – as in the heart of a black hole, for example, or in the Big Bang in which the

Universe was created – and where space and time cease to exist. In a black hole, the singularity is 'veiled' by an event horizon from which no information can escape. Some scientists, supporters of the 'cosmic censorship' theory, believe that this is *always* the case – nature always hides its singularities. Others, however, believe that singularities can sometimes become visible: theorist Stephen Hawkins has shown that black holes gradually 'evaporate' to expose the singularities – naked singularities – at their hearts, and some scientists believe that when matter rotates too fast to become a normal black hole, it can become visible from certain directions – that is, it does not form an event horizon.

Now *if* a naked singularity exists in the Universe, then it is possible, according to the

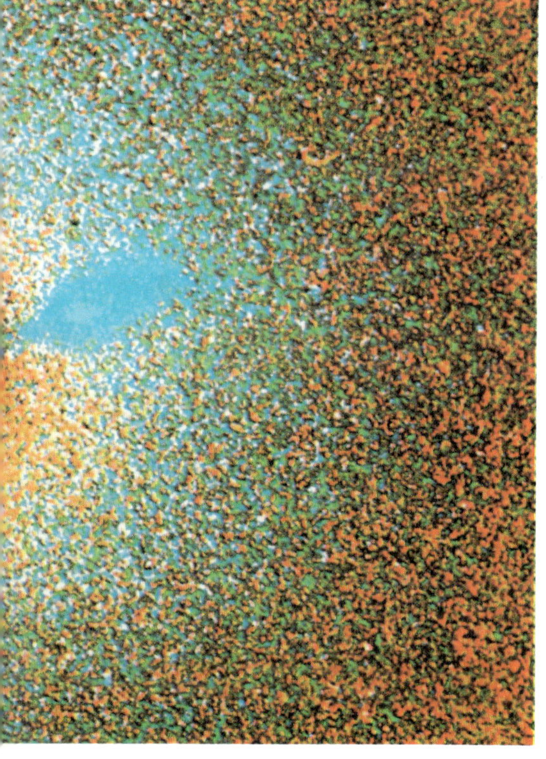

Two possible sites for black holes. In the computer-processed image of M87, one of the largest galaxies known (left), a hot bright jet of matter, emitted from the galaxy's core, can be seen. The jet sends out enormous quantities of energy in the form of light and radio waves. The source of the energy may be a black hole at the galaxy's centre. The same explanation has been invoked for the enormous explosion that is occurring at the centre of the galaxy M82 in Ursa Major (below). Like all proposed black hole identifications, these are highly controversial

laws of physics, to travel in an orbit 'around' the singularity – an orbit that takes you first into the future or past, then back home to the time and place you started from. Such an orbit is called a *closed timelike line* – and, of course, it implies the possibility of time travel and all the philosophical problems it entails. It is small wonder that it has caused dissension among the scientists. One school of thought believes that, because naked singularities imply the existence of closed timelike lines, naked singularities cannot exist. Another group of theorists points out that the Big Bang in which the Universe was born may have been a bursting out from a singularity, like a black hole in reverse; thus at least one naked singularity may not only have existed, but may have been the cause of our Universe coming into existence. And if a naked singularity once existed, inside the

Universe, then, because the closed timelike lines associated with it remain fixed for all time, it influences the whole future of space-time. If we could only find it, we would have a ready-made time machine with which we could visit any time since the beginning of the Universe.

But most startling of all are the ideas of a maverick American theorist, that not only may closed timelike lines exist, but it might one day be possible for mankind to *create* them. With 20th-century physics and engineering as his guide, Frank Tipler has sketched out plans that a future civilisation might use as a blueprint in building a time machine.

Tipler's work, published in respectable journals such as the *Physical Review* and *Annals of Physics*, is necessarily highly mathematical and not always easy for the uninitiated to follow. But when asked straight out 'Is time travel possible?', he replied: 'My current view is that there is indeed a real theoretical possibility for causality violation in the context of relativity theory.' Remember that, in scientific terms, 'causality violation' implies 'time travel'! The tricky mathematical part of Tipler's work is the calculation that time travel is allowed within the laws of relativity theory. The Universe does 'allow' time travel after all, and there is no known reason why closed timelike lines should not exist in the real world. The next question Tipler looked at was whether the conditions appropriate for time travel to take place could arise naturally in the Universe. Finally, he has looked at the possibility of building an artificial time machine.

The crucial factor, Tipler discovered, is the existence – or creation – of a massive, rotating object. A large amount of matter concentrated in one place distorts the fabric of space-time by the force of gravity. If the object also rotates, then space-time is twisted still more by the rotation, as the firm grip of gravity tries to carry the fabric of space-time round with the rotating mass. For some

combinations of mass, density and angular velocity a singularity can be formed without creating an event horizon. The region of distorted space-time around this naked singularity is called, logically enough, the 'strong field' region, referring to the gravitational field. Tipler has proved that a traveller from a weak field region – the Earth, say – could go to a strong field region near such a rotating object, move in the direction of negative time, and then return home to the weak field region without ever violating any known physical law. He would return to find himself in the past, returning to Earth, if he wished, before he left. Building a time machine is impracticable now. But that may not always be the case.

A working time machine can be constructed, in principle, by taking a sufficiently massive but compact lump of material – any material – and making it spin fast enough. Strictly speaking, the rotating material ought

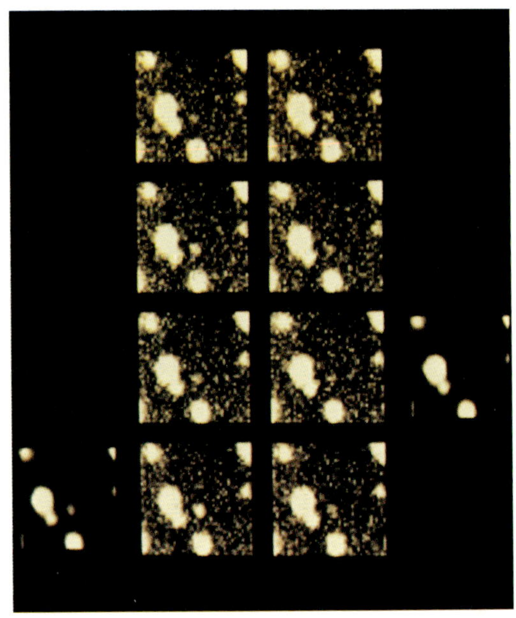

Right: a pulsar lying among stars in the constellation of Vela flashes on and off. These pictures were made with sensitive electronic detectors connected to a telescope. 'Noise', similar to television interference, obscures the original eight pictures The computer-enhanced pictures flanking the central sequence show the pulsar at maximum and minimum brightness. In the left-hand picture it is a faint dot just below the centre that is absent in the right-hand picture. Theoretically pulsars could be harnessed in the future for purposes of travel forwards and backwards through time

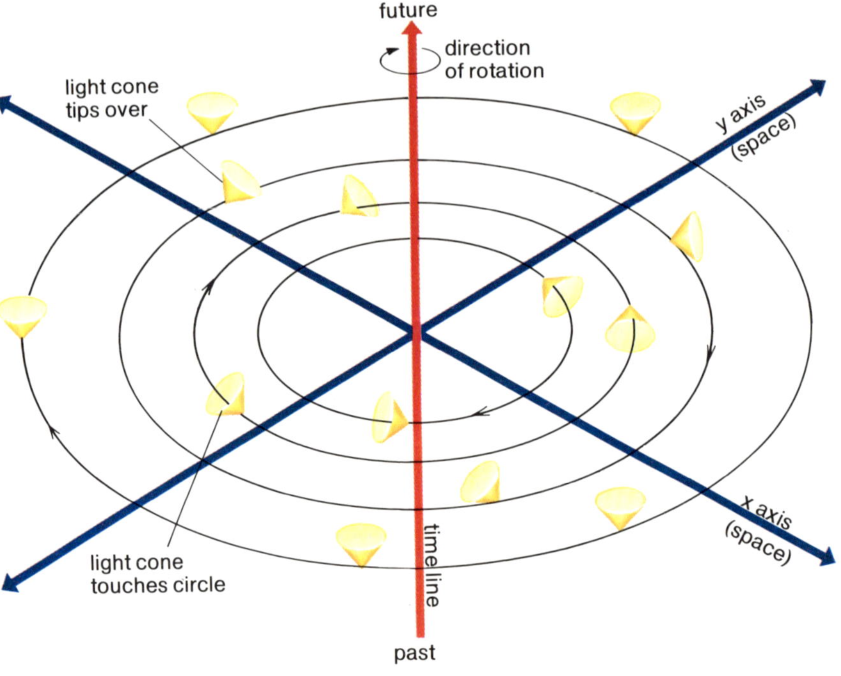

In space-time diagrams two space dimensions are shown; the third represents time. The 'light cones' (left) represent a light wave converging and spreading out again. Only journeys within cones (that is, slower than light) are possible. But near a massive rotating object (below) light cones are tilted. Journeys can lie within a cone, yet go backwards in time

1960s, astronomers discovered sources of rapidly pulsing radiation in our Galaxy. These sources, dubbed pulsars, are now explained as rapidly rotating neutron stars. Some of them spin at a rate of once very few milliseconds; most have a mass about the same as our Sun. Of course, the spin isn't quite fast enough to make them time machines, and these spinning neutron stars are not stretched into elongated cylinders. But the description of a pulsar is tantalisingly close to Frank Tipler's description of a working time machine.

Here, perhaps, is the way some future spacefaring civilisation might set about making a time machine. First, choose a suitable pulsar. Stretch it into an elongated cylinder, increase its spin appropriately, and you can open for business. There are just two remaining snags. First, such a time machine

to be in the form of an infinitely long cylinder, but Tipler believes that a cylinder 10 times longer than its diameter probably has the right proportions to do the trick. How much mass do you need? Astronomers know that in the last stage of compression before the black hole state, objects called neutron stars exist in the Universe. Such a star might contain as much matter as our Sun, packed into a volume no more than 15 miles (24 kilometres) across; the name 'neutron star' tells us that the density of such a star is roughly the same as the density of neutrons in the heart of an atom. A neutron star is, in effect, a whole star compressed to the density of an atomic nucleus. Keeping the mass of the Sun as an approximate guide, our working time machine could be made from a neutron star squeezed into the shape of a cylinder 7 miles (10 kilometres) across and 70 miles (100 kilometres) long, rotating twice every millisecond, with the rim of the cylinder moving at half the speed of light.

It sounds outrageous. But in the late

remain. One of the shortest stories ever published by science-fiction writer Larry Niven has the title 'Rotating cylinders and the possibility of global causality violation'. Niven stole the title, he acknowledges, from one of Tipler's erudite articles in the *Physical Review*. The story describes a future civilisation that tries to take Tipler's work to its logical conclusion and build a working time machine. Every time the work nears completion, some catastrophe strikes the builders. The punch line comes when another race discovers a half-built time machine and decides to finish the job; at the moment the leader of the civilisation decides to proceed with the project, the sun in the sky of his planet blows up as a nova and his civilisation is destroyed.

Violating causality

Niven's frightening story highlights the implication of the argument that causality violation is abhorrent to nature, taken to its logical conclusion. The illogicality of the story may be a kind of double bluff, representing Niven's own attempt to make us, the readers, say 'but that's ridiculous', leaving us with the only possible alternative – that causality violation really is possible after all. Tipler, cautiously, says only that 'we are a very long way from completely resolving the causality violation question.' But that, coming from a respected mathematical physicist with a thorough knowledge of Einstein's theories, speaks volumes. At the very least, if anyone ever tells you flatly that 'time travel is impossible', you can be sure that he doesn't know what he is talking about. The fairest answer modern science can give to the question, 'Is time travel possible?' is 'We don't know.' And that, of course, means that perhaps it is possible to travel in time after all.

works only from the moment of its creation. Once it is made, you can use it to go forward in time and return to your starting time, but you can never go back to a time before the naked singularity came into being. Secondly, says Tipler, time travel might need rather a lot of energy. If you imagine sending a physical object on a closed timelike loop so that it ends up alongside itself, then in effect you have created a duplicate of the original object. Einstein's equations tells us that mass is equivalent to energy, according to the familiar equation $E = mc^2$. Creating amount m of mass requires energy mc^2, and c is the speed of light, 186,000 miles per second (300,000 km/h). So Tipler believes that a working time machine could most probably be used in practice only to send messages, not material bodies, through time. On the other hand, a civilisation capable of sculpting neutron stars into time machines might have energy enough to squander on physical time travel as well.

The problems of causality violation

Above: *How they met themselves*, by Dante Gabriel Rossetti. The startled couple encounter apparitions of themselves – but time travellers could meet their physical selves according to Frank Tipler's theory

Right: Dr Who, one of the most famous of fictional time travellers, with his somewhat impractical design of time machine

Left: engraving after Breughel's *The triumph of time*, showing the medieval obsession with the remorseless march of time and the inevitability of death. Fate, in the shape of a cart carrying the signs of the zodiac, crushes beneath it the pathetic detritus of Man's material aspirations – treasure chests, crowns, musical instruments – while the Grim Reaper and the Angel of Judgement bring up the rear. Such paintings were known as *memento mori*, or reminders of death, which comes to all, high or low. When life was bleak, hard and often brutal time was seen as the tyrant pushing Man to his doom

When time slips

Everyone is aware of the passing of time; we grow old and die, and there is no 'turning the clock back'. But as JOAN FORMAN points out, time can sometimes behave in strange and uncharacteristic ways

WE TAKE SO MUCH for granted in our lives on this planet that it requires a major shock to awake us from our usual state of unthinking acceptance. One little-questioned area of experience is that of time, for we are conditioned from cradle to grave to accept it in a certain form – that of chronology or the time of the clock.

From babyhood the days, months and years are measured out for us. We are taught 'to tell the time', by which is meant the time recorded by the nearest clock. We learn to interpret the calendar – which month is May, which September, and when the seasons begin and end. Yet all this time-telling is merely a convenience, a human device originated to enable primitive Man to know when to feed livestock, plant seed and harvest crops. The clock and calendar are mechanisms only, to help us order our lives and impose a routine on chaos. But chronology may not be the only form of time; the cosmos itself may produce a temporal mechanism of an entirely different nature.

It is likely that the conflict of this cosmic or universal time with man-made chronology is the cause of the extraordinary phenomenon known as timeslips, where two aspects or dimensions of time seem to operate at once, and the subject is likely to find himself living in the present and the past (or

Right: the shop in Great Yarmouth, England, where 'Mr Squirrel' went to buy plastic envelopes in which to keep his coin collection – and stepped into another age

in some cases, the present and the future) simultaneously. The experience is at best puzzling, and can occasionally be disorientating and alarming.

When the author was researching her book on the subject, *The mask of time*, some extraordinary experiences came to light of timeslips that deal with the past. Take for instance the case of the Norfolk man who shall be called Mr Squirrel. The hobby of this elderly man is coin-collecting and, like many amateur numismatists, he uses small plastic envelopes as coin receptacles. It was sometime in 1973 that he decided to visit a shop in Great Yarmouth, Norfolk which, he had heard, sold suitable envelopes. He knew the whereabouts of the shop but had never visited it, so that when he reached the place, the cobbled space in front of it and the brightly painted façade made an impression on him. He also took in the interior details. There were photograph frames with flower motifs upon them, an old-fashioned till-box, and a container full of walking sticks. Before he could examine the place further, the assistant appeared, and Mr Squirrel noticed that she wore a long black skirt and a blouse he described as having 'mutton-chop sleeves'. The girl's hair was piled on top of her head in a large bun.

Since this was 1973, a time of variety in women's dress, with long skirts and period-type costume appearing frequently for day wear, the old gentleman was unperturbed. He asked the young assistant for envelopes for his coins, and she produced these from a brown box full of the objects. When he remarked upon their number, she replied that the men on the sailing ships bought them to use as receptacles for fish-hooks. Somewhat surprised, her customer nevertheless took his purchase, paying for them in decimal coinage. The shop girl asked for a 'shilling' – which did not surprise the elderly man, who still thought in terms of the old coins. He gave her a 5p piece at which she looked in astonishment but made no comment. One feature of the transaction had puzzled him: there had been total silence

inside the shop when he was in it, and an absence of any traffic sound from outside.

A week later he returned for a further supply of envelopes, and had the shock of his life when he approached the shop. It appeared to be a totally different place from that of the week before: the cobbles had become pavement, the exterior and interior of the shop were dark and weathered, and the fixtures were not as they had been. Strangest of all, the shop assistant was a mature woman and denied any knowledge of the young girl he had seen the previous week. Worse was to come, for she met with a blank negative his request for further envelopes. Their shop had never stocked them, she said. The shop's manager supported her in this statement. The only evidence the old man had that he had ever bought anything was the few small envelopes purchased the previous week. The old-fashioned street and the shop with its Edwardian assistant and merchandise had disappeared as though they had never been.

The possible date of the envelopes was later checked with the manufacturers – who said that bags of such a type were first used in the 1920s, though the method of manufacture was perfected before the First World War. This was a particularly strange, inconclusive case of slipping time, of the apparent impingement of time past upon the present.

Return of time past

A striking instance of a past slip occurred to Mrs Turrell-Clarke, a one time resident of Wisley-cum-Pyrford in Surrey, where her experience took place. The lady was cycling down the modern road on her way to evensong in her village church, when abruptly the road appeared to become a field path and she seemed to be walking along it. Coming towards her she saw a man in the peasant dress of the 13th century, and he stood to one side to allow her to pass. She felt herself at the time to be wearing a nun's robes.

A month later this lady sat in the same parish church (it had formerly been a small chapel attached to nearby Newark Abbey, and had miraculously survived the dissolution of the monasteries), joining with the choir in singing a plainsong hymn. Halfway through the chant, she saw to her astonishment the church 'change' to its original state – earth floor, stone altar, lancet windows – and processing around the centre space were brown-habited monks, intoning the same plainsong chant that occupied the 20th-century choir. Yet at this moment of apprehension, Mrs Turrell-Clarke also knew herself to be one of a small group of people at the back of the church, taking little part in the proceedings.

On enquiry, this lady found that the monks of Newark Abbey wore black habits and could not be the figures of her experience. However, in the year 1293, the monks of Westminster Abbey had apparently been granted the use of the chapel, and

Pyrford Church, Surrey, where Mrs Turrell-Clarke attended evensong and, while listening to the choir, suddenly found herself back in the 13th-century church, listening to monks chanting the same plainsong as the 20th-century choir. Although the timeslip lasted only a few moments, the details of the scene in the old church remained vividly in her memory. When she came to check them against historical documents she found them surprisingly accurate they were indeed a brown-habited order.

Another startling experience was reported by Mrs Louisa Hand. It concerned the hamlet of Cockey Moore, near Bury, Lancashire, and visits that this lady paid in childhood to her grandmother's cottage, which was the first of a row in the hamlet. Louisa was at the time aged about nine and old enough not to mistake one dwelling for another.

A curious cottage

The child had been playing in front of the houses when she decided to go in, and ran back through the open door of her grandmother's cottage, only to find herself in a strange environment. The furniture was different and older, the kitchen doorway had disappeared entirely, and everything seemed darker than usual and unnaturally quiet.

Thinking she had mistaken the house, the girl ran out to check. This time she made certain of the right door before re-entering; yet again found herself in the same strange surroundings as before. She went out immediately, puzzled and uneasy. After several minutes she again entered the same cottage, and this time found everything as she remembered it. One of her aunts was at work in the kitchen. Normality had returned.

There seems little doubt that the child had walked into the cottage's past. But how? What mechanism was involved? She seemed to 'cross a threshold', remarking, as she did, the quality of silence just as did Mr Squirrel. Louisa also noticed the darker aspect of the room, but this is accountable; the amount of light admitted to houses has increased as windows have become larger. The dislocation seems to have been abrupt as was the transition back into the present. From one dimension into another? Maybe. Maybe not.

On 29 May 1973, a Norwich teacher, Mrs Anne May, and her husband visited the Clava Cairns in Inverness, a group of three

A monolith of the Clava Cairns, Inverness, Bronze Age burial site. When a visitor leaned back against it she experienced a timeslip in which she apparently witnessed the cairns being built nearly 2000 years ago

burial cairns dating from the Early Bronze Age, *c*.1800–1500 BC. The day was crisp, bright, and lively with birdsong, and Mrs May first walked around the cairns, then turned to the circles of monoliths surrounding each. Finally she leaned against a stone belonging to the north-eastern cairn, and briefly closed her eyes in an attempt at the yogi's 'slipped second' (a moment of complete blankness). When she opened them, she saw a group of men, wearing shaggy tunics and, she thought, cross-gartered trousers. They were moving forward slowly, apparently dragging one of the huge monoliths over the ground. She particularly noticed the figures' long dark hair. This curious vision might have persisted, had not a party of tourists entered the glade. At once she was back in the 20th century.

This is a particularly clear example of what appears to happen in timeslips. The

---

Alternative views of time include those of J. W. Dunne, whose pioneering work in this field was first expressed in *An experiment with time*. Dunne's attitude was revolutionary for the 1920s, stating as it did that chronology was not the only form that time can take.

Most of his theories were based on the evidence of his dreams, which were frequently precognitive and often related to subsequent events as reported in newspapers. By keeping a record of his dreams Dunne came to realise that they were a blend of past, present and future.

Although he realised he had made a major discovery, he made the mistake of thinking his experience unique. And although he grasped the concept of precognition, he failed to understand it and pursued the idea of time as a dimension

Two views of time

that led ultimately into a dead end.

It was Dunne's work, however, that inspired the second great time-enquirer of the 20th century, the writer J. B. Priestley (left). He saw time as a divided process in three segments: Time One – clock time; Time Two – the time of the possible future; and Time Three – the time of the creative imagination. His book *Man and time*, written in the 1940s, contains fascinating insights into the possible nature of time. He claimed that chronological time is only an invention to explain the way events follow one another – that is, it is a concept that is dependent on the idea of causality. And if, as C.G. Jung suggested, *acausality* is one of the ruling principles of the Universe, there is no reason why time should not play all the tricks it pleases.

subject was interested in her surroundings but not concentrating upon them; the 'slip' occurred at a precise place and moment – when her body touched the monolith – and the transition from present to past was immediate, as was its reversal.

The author had a similar experience when visiting Haddon Hall in Derbyshire, during research for *The mask of time*. She was not concerned with work, for this was a holiday visit to a house she had always hoped to see. She had paused in the courtyard before the house, considering its architecture, the entrance door and the flight of steps up to it, when without warning she 'saw' a group of four children playing at the top of the steps – a small child, two older boys and a still older girl of about nine. The latter had her back to her and she could see only shoulder-length blonde hair, a white Dutch hat and a long green-grey silk dress with a lace collar. The children were laughing helplessly as at some huge joke and the author watched fascinated, fully aware that she was not seeing with the physical eye, yet equally conscious of watching real action. Then the elder girl turned to face her. She had expected a little beauty and saw instead extreme plainness: broad face, snub nose, wide jaw. Startled, she took a step forward; and at once the scene vanished. She was left with the memory of the laughter and the elder girl's happy, plain face.

The author toured the house looking for a portrait, for she was sure that the eldest child at least belonged to Haddon. Among the ancestral paintings that hung on the panelled walls was one of a blonde child wearing a Dutch hat and a grey-green silk dress with a lace collar. The baby's face was that of the girl she had seen outside, the wide jawline unmistakable. She was, said the custodian when asked, Lady Grace Manners.

Again there is a trigger factor as in Anne May's case. She leaned against a certain stone, the author stood upon a certain spot, and when she moved from it the picture vanished. Throughout these past slips the 'trigger' is frequently present.

Some past slips appear to relate to possible reincarnation experiences, others to what was once considered a type of haunting. All seem to be natural in their operation in that they apparently have some connection with the human electromagnetic field.

So time is not at all a matter of clocks and watches. Indeed they have little to do with the 'real' time of the Universe.

The courtyard of Haddon Hall, Derbyshire, where author Joan Forman saw some children from the house's past engaged in a hilarious game. The 'vision' seemed to be triggered by standing on a certain spot, like flicking a switch to show an old film

Leaps into the future

To find oneself abruptly in the future – however briefly – is a disconcerting, but strangely common, experience. This chapter presents more evidence for the bizarre phenomenon of timeslips

RESEARCHERS INTO the curious phenomenon known as timeslips frequently begin their study with the assumption that the majority of cases would refer to time past – that is, where the present suddenly gives way to a different time dimension and the past is experienced. But even a cursory glance at the vast file of reported cases would prove such researchers wrong.

Future timeslips seem almost as common as those belonging to the past, although frequently they appear to cause those who experience them more alarm, perhaps because they cannot be explained away as prior knowledge.

Precognitive experiences appear to fall into one of two categories: waking premonition or precognition, and precognitive dreams. The latter in turn may include recurrent dreams forecasting the future, but single dreams are more common. The subject matter may be of a trivial or a tragic nature. Curiously perhaps, the dramatic events in life seem to have no priority in the mechanism, but occur in about the same proportion as those dealing with trivia.

Take the case of a Cheshire teacher who shall be called Mrs Xenia Stafford. In June 1948 she dreamed that she was packing a trunk with clothes that she removed from a nearby wardrobe. 'Taking clothes I did not possess from a wardrobe I had never seen to put into a trunk I didn't own,' as she described it. She was to become a student at Manchester University the following

Above: the legendary prophetess Mother Shipton. Born in a cave at Knaresborough, Yorkshire, in 1488, she soon gained a reputation as a seeress – someone who literally sees the future as it will happen

Below: Compton Wynyates, Warwickshire, England. It was this beautiful stately home that featured in the dreams of one woman for 20 years before she visited it

autumn, but at the time of the dream had not even begun to think of what she would need by way of clothes and did not possess a trunk of any sort.

In the September following her dream an uncle bought her a trunk from a lost-property sale in London; her mother made and bought her a selection of new clothes and eventually she moved into a Hall of Residence for female students. She found that her new room-mate had commandeered the best bed and wardrobe and she, Xenia, was left with an old triangular wardrobe, which she did not at the time 'recognise'.

It was not until the end of that first term, when she found herself packing her trunk beside the wardrobe, that she recalled the dream of six months earlier, and recognised the details as identical. A small-scale but significant experience.

Another dream giving trivial precognitive information occurred to Mrs M. Bussell, who at the time was working in Gray's Inn Road, London, and regularly used the Underground from her home in Stockwell to Chancery Lane.

Curiously trivial

In the early hours of one morning she dreamed that she was ascending the steps of Chancery Lane Underground station, as she usually did, and that as she climbed the steps on the right hand side, she happened to glance across to the flight on the left. Coming down them she saw a middle-aged woman with a crippled leg, which caused her to descend with great slowness and caution.

Mrs Bussell awoke at this point, and felt somewhat irritated by the apparent pointlessness of the dream. Had she varied her route to work that morning, the memory

might have gone from her mind. However, she went as usual via Chancery Lane tube station, and as she climbed the right hand flight of steps she chanced to glance to her left. Descending the left hand flight was the very woman of that morning's dream, walking down with extreme care on account of a crippled leg.

The subject could make no sense of the incident; she had never seen the woman before – nor did she again. The dream had merely announced an event some hours ahead of its taking place. No sequel occurred, no meaning attached to it; it was a piece of simple precognition only.

Finding dream houses

It is not uncommon for dreams to feature specific places that are at the time unknown to the dreamer. The scene may then be encountered later, and the dream thereupon regarded as precognitive. However, this need not be the case. The mind appears often to register information subconsciously through pictures seen in waking life and afterwards forgotten save for a dream. Then when the actual place is encountered in 'real life' it is believed to have been announced precognitively by the dream.

Occasionally such place-recognition is encountered in the form of a recurrent dream: a correspondent described to the present writer a dream she had had since childhood of a 'Tudor-style country mansion built as a square' set in a fine garden with grassy banks. The dream recurred every year, but it was not until she stayed in Leamington Spa in Warwickshire that she visited the beautiful house of Compton Wynyates and recognised it at once as the subject of her dream.

It should be noted again that nothing of importance occurred to this dreamer in connection with the house, and why it should have stalked her dreams for some 20 years is incomprehensible. However, perhaps one of the mistakes we make is in thinking that all apparently paranormal events are bound to have significance. The truth seems to be otherwise; some strange happenings have significance that is recognisable sooner or later, others do not. They occur impartially.

The incidence of precognitive dreams is exceeded by waking precognition. This is extremely common, is almost always involuntary and frequently only a short time ahead of the event it heralds. It seems to be predictive rather than premonitory, concerning minor rather than major events. However, when dramatic events are predicted, they are usually precise and unmistakable. It is also more common for the development time – that is, the time between the precognitive experience and its fulfilment – to be short-term, a matter of hours or days rather than weeks or months. Yet cases do exist where the precognition has been exceedingly long term.

One of the most striking instances of

precognition of a dramatic event occurred to Miss R. H. Hodgskin of Birmingham and her friend, who shall be called Tessa G. On 20 April 1974 the two were spending some time in London and decided to visit the Tower, which is – perhaps of all London's monuments – the most emotive, with its mixed history of royalty, pageantry, pain and terror. However on the day of the two friends' visit all was peaceful and the White Tower (their immediate goal) housed only the armoury and a number of tourists like themselves.

Having spent some time inspecting the

Horrific sounds from the future were heard by 'Tessa G.' when she visited the Tower of London. Although her companion heard nothing, Tessa's distress was obvious as she perceived the anguished screams and cries of many children. At the time, she thought the sounds were from the Tower's unhappy past, but on 17 July 1974 – four months after Tessa's experience – a terrorist bomb exploded at the Tower, injuring 33 people, many of them young children. Yeoman warders help the victims (above) while police and firemen assess the damage to the historic White Tower (right). Reading about the bomb, Tessa was sure she had heard the cries of the maimed children

weapons the pair began to find the atmosphere of the dungeons oppressive and decided to return to the open air. They were half-way up the steps, when Tessa turned to her friend and said, 'I can hear children shouting.' Miss Hodgskin could hear nothing but a faint murmur of conversation from below, and said so. Tessa became agitated and her voice rose. 'No,' she said, 'I can hear children shouting and screaming.' Her friend could still hear nothing unusual, and each was inclined to doubt the evidence of the other's senses. However, Tessa G. was obviously convinced that she heard the children's cries and was deeply disturbed by them. Eventually the deadlock was resolved by a return to the light in search of a restorative cup of tea. The affair was then put out of their minds for the time being.

It was a few months later that a terrorist bomb planted in the armoury of the White Tower exploded, killing and seriously injuring a number of people, including several children.

What was it that Tessa G. heard? A sound of pain and terror from the Tower's dismal past? Or the agony of children who would suffer in that place some months ahead of her experience? In the circumstances, the latter view seems most likely, although there is no means of proving or disproving the matter without having heard both the hallucinatory and the actual sounds.

It is apparent that in precognitive as in retrocognitive occurrences, the experience may be either heard or seen, with occasional combinations of the two.

A vanishing launderette

Two television series based on the concept of timeslips were produced by the BBC, Eastern Region, and these in turn gave rise to a flood of letters from viewers with time experiences of their own to report. One particularly interesting case came from a teacher in Holt, Norfolk; while involved in a slight traffic contretemps in that town, he happened to notice that a nearby launderette that had been under construction for some time was now completed and in use by the public. He reported the fact to his wife on his return home, but when she took laundry there later in the day she was puzzled to find that she had made a journey in vain. The launderette, though seen in its completed and bustling state by her husband some hours earlier, was actually still unfinished, full of dust and workmen, as it had been for several months.

It was six weeks after this incident that the place was actually opened to the public for use; therefore the Norfolk teacher had seen the completed shop several weeks ahead of his own moment in time. Such experiences are, to say the least, disorientating, and leave the subject doubting the workings of his own brain. However, it may well be that it is the brain itself that is acting as transformer and interpreter of information coming from the future.

Precognitive information does not always have meaning for the person who experiences it. Occasionally it relates only obliquely to the subject. Take, for instance, the case of a cousin of Mrs E. H. of Bourne End.

Before 1939, this cousin knew slightly a young man who was the boy friend of one of her girl friends. At the outbreak of war he joined the RAF and was soon on active service. Several months later the cousin had what she thought was a waking dream, in which she saw clear mental images but knew herself not to be asleep. These images were of a life raft

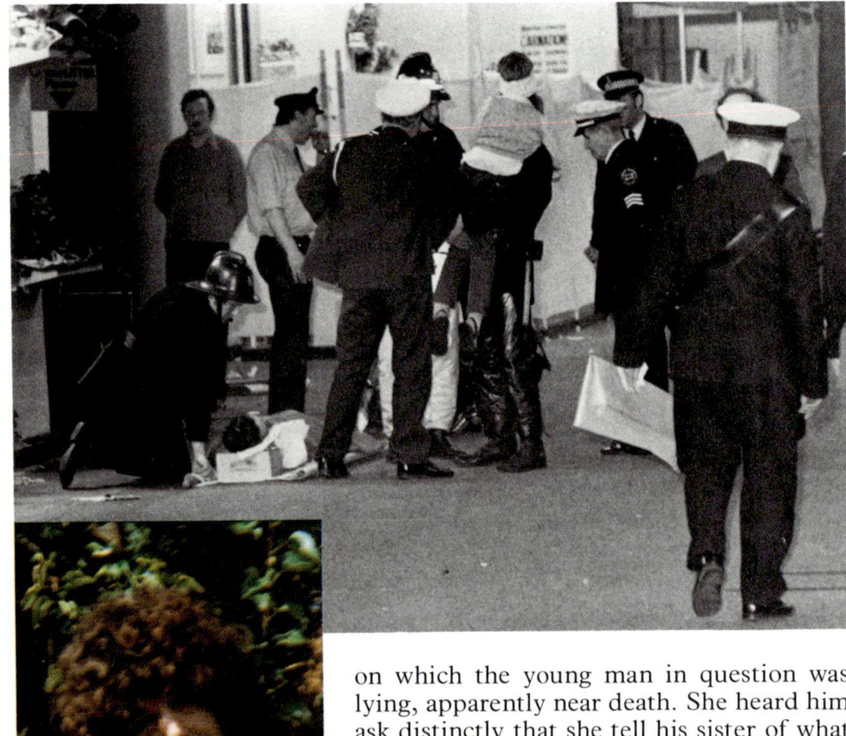

Top: the injured are tended by officers of the emergency services after a bomb exploded at the Ideal Home Exhibition at Olympia, London, 27 March 1976

Above: Margaret Baker, a psychic from East Anglia who had twice seen 'real' placards at newspaper stands announcing the Olympia bomb disaster – but several months before it happened. When the exhibition opened she felt a sense of impending doom, and warned a colleague not to visit it. A day before the explosion she 'saw' the bomb being placed in a litter bin and heard screams. When she saw the subsequent television report it substantiated her 'vision' in every detail

on which the young man in question was lying, apparently near death. She heard him ask distinctly that she tell his sister of what had happened – that he had been shot down and drifting on the life raft for two days. A few days later she ran into this very young man, who was on leave in London, and was relieved to see him perfectly well and normal. He had apparently had no adverse experiences at this stage. The young woman dismissed the matter as 'just a silly dream'.

More than two years passed before she read in the paper of his death. He had been found dead on a life raft and had apparently been there for some considerable time. On enquiry, she discovered that he had indeed had a sister, but the latter had recently died. The cousin's 'message', therefore, could not be delivered.

This is a curious case, both on account of the long time-lag between vision and event, and because of the very slight connection between the subject and the apparent transmitter (the airman) of the information. Mrs E. H.'s cousin seemingly 'picked up' the details of this distant event, apparently at the will of the airman himself, and the information seems to have been intended for transmission – a fascinating example of this type of long-range foretelling.

The incidence of precognition is widespread. Prediction has a history almost as long as that of the human race, and prophets have always had some honour (though alas, not always in their own country). Indeed, when prophecies have been gloomy (and accurate), seeing the future has often proved downright dangerous. However, precognition still occurs and does not appear to be subject to human control. Perhaps one day we *could* learn to control it.

Time out of mind

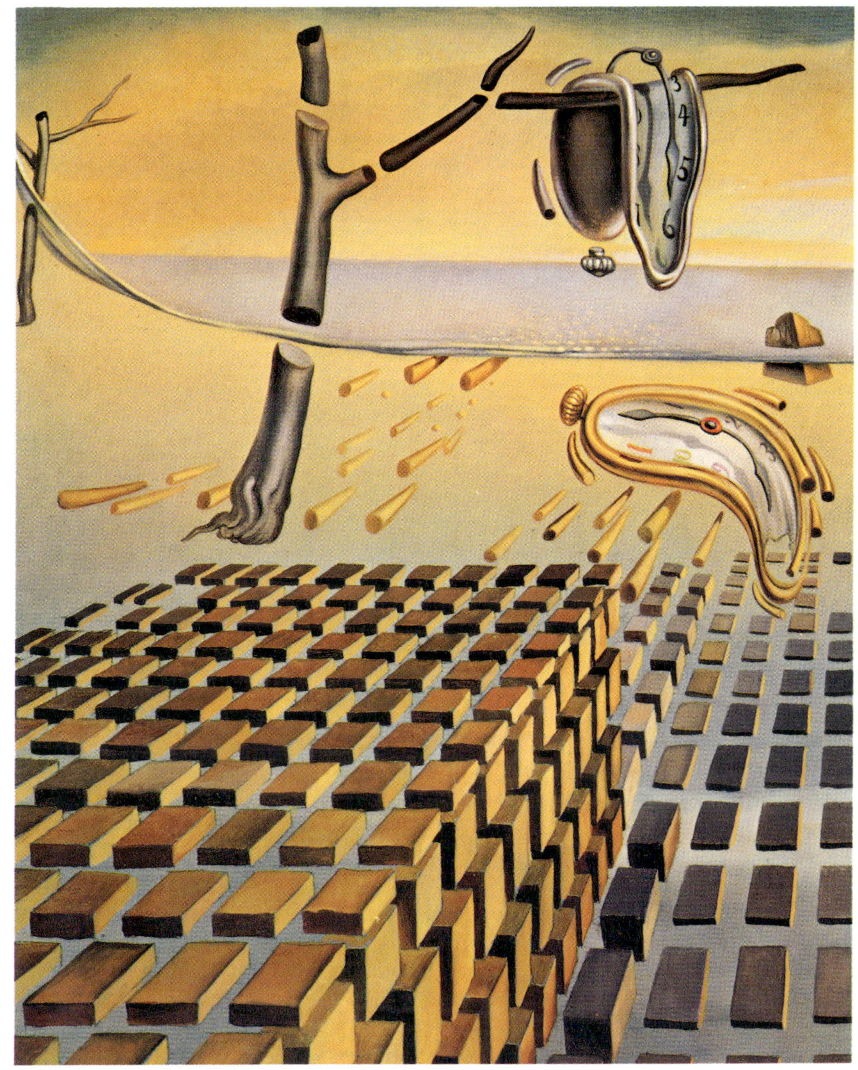

1. A trigger factor that appears to set the occurrence in motion.
2. Abrupt onset of the experience.
3. A sensation of living in two time zones at once, either past and present or future and present.
4. A feeling of being an integral part of the experience or a participant in the action.
5. A noticeable absence of sound from beginning to end of the timeslip.
6. A marked difference is frequently mentioned between normal light conditions and those experienced during the timeslip. A 'silvery light' is often described.

An electric experience

From the above it seems that certain physical effects take place; the subject sees and hears abnormally and experiences a feeling of disorientation or detachment. Occasionally, people have reported a tingling sensation or nausea immediately before they experienced a timeslip, just as particularly sensitive people may react to an impending earthquake or thunderstorm. (It is interesting that several of the sensations described can also herald hauntings or other paranormal happenings.) One subject wrote describing 'a tingling in arms and legs; a feeling of being "plugged in".' She may have been very near the truth for there are indications that some form of electrical activity plays a part in many paranormal experiences.

A 'plugging in' or trigger was a major factor in the case of Mrs Anne May, the Norwich teacher who, in May 1973, at Clava Cairns in Scotland experienced a slip into what appeared to be the remote past of the

If we could find ways of analysing the timeslip phenomenon, we might also discover some tantalising clues to the nature of reality itself. But how could we begin this formidable task?

TO MOST PEOPLE timeslips – if they think about them at all – are firmly relegated to the realm of 'the supernatural' and left at that. But the 'supernatural' cannot exist, since any event arising in the natural Universe in which we live must have natural origins. If we cannot explain any phenomenon in terms of the known laws of nature, then this must be because our current knowledge of those laws is incomplete. Who could explain the mechanism of an eclipse before the true motions of the planets were known?

But the mechanism of timeslips eludes us still; we can only sift the evidence and search for some common denominators among the experiences – and possibly some relationship with known laws of physics. So far these common factors have been discovered:

Above: a detail from *Disintegration of the persistence of memory* by Salvador Dali. The nightmare scene is festooned with melting clocks that represent the ultimate non-existence of man-made time

Right: a 19th-century mandarin's court observes an eclipse. The scientific view it enthusiastically through a telescope while the superstitious fearfully hide their faces. Like eclipses, timeslips may one day be understood

Captain Flowerdew (inset) who, as a child, picked up a pink pebble from a beach and instantly 'remembered' a desert city built of pinkish stone where 'he' had died in a battle centuries ago. Detailed as the memory was, it was not until he saw a television programme about the ancient site of Petra (above) that he remembered the city's name

area (see page 88). Significantly, it was not until she leaned back against one of the standing stones that the extraordinary transition into the past took place, as though a switch had been thrown. Several correspondents have used that very phrase in describing their individual timeslips. And the immediacy of the slip is always pronounced. It is as though the trigger object (in Anne May's case, the stone) itself contained the power to evoke the time dislocation.

This may not be so far-fetched as it sounds, for if the operation of timeslips is due to the transmitting of information from past or future into the present, then that information must already be in existence somewhere. Perhaps every single component of the world in which we live is continually broadcasting information about itself (its form, colour, texture, situation, and so on) by means of 'waves' as yet unknown to science. Some of this information may be received and absorbed by surrounding material and, when conditions are appropriate, rebroadcast by the receiver. Any human being then in the area whose own brain is at the time operating on the same frequency as the transmitter may register an audio or visual impression of the original 'wave' pattern sent forth by the first broadcaster. Thus we ourselves in moments of high emotion or stress may be sending out signals into the air that will be received years hence by some sensitive individual. Most (though perhaps not all) hauntings can probably be attributed to this type of mechanism.

What are these mysterious waves that have the power to carry pictures and sounds through time? We do not know. But it is a physical fact that all objects radiate electromagnetic waves. Light waves, which enable us to perceive the world around us, are just one example; radio waves, infra-red and ultra-violet waves, x-rays and gamma rays are all electromagnetic. Most of these invisible radiations were discovered within the last century; who can say what further kinds of radiation await discovery?

The fascinating branch of physics called quantum mechanics posits the concept of electrons in atoms (and our Universe is constructed on the atom) moving backwards and forwards in time equally easily. Perhaps, therefore, it is possible for information from the future to be returned to the present by some, as yet, totally unknown mechanism.

The future is now

But, if such information can be returned from the future, then that future must already exist 'somewhere', in some form. And it may be that we ourselves – and indeed all atomic material – carry within us the seeds of our own future.

The behaviour of individual atomic particles is unpredictable, but it is possible to predict how they will behave *en masse*. In other words, by cause and effect all events seem to be predetermined. Perhaps the idea of destiny arose from an instinctive knowledge of this very fact: that we are what we are and do what we do because we are constructed genetically in a certain way.

If this were always and wholly true, we and the whole of human history would indeed be predestined and our futures would be laid down for us inescapably. However, it appears that we do have the power to alter and modify our 'destiny' – at least occasionally – by the exercise of our will.

Therefore when we encounter precognitive experiences, whether dreaming or waking, it may be that we are receiving from matter already existing (people, animals, buildings and so on) information about its own future development. In the short term such information is likely to prove true, in the long term less so, for over a longer period of time there is greater likelihood of human will being used to intervene in the cause and effect – the causality – process. With more time available there are more opportunities for action – and therefore more opportunities for change.

However, there are exceptions. Occasionally precognitive experiences will come to completion accurately several years after they have been encountered. There are two known cases where there was a full 20-year lapse between the experience and its accurate fulfilment.

This is, however, unusual. Past slips cannot always be explained as 'recordings' of past events, though doubtless this mechanism accounts for a great number. Several persons have reported finding themselves

The girl from Scotland

One afternoon in 1950 Brigadier K. Treseder and colleagues from the British and American embassies in Oslo, Norway, went skiing.

On preparing to return, the Brigadier, his wife and a friend were separated from the others. They were suddenly confronted by a tall old lady dressed in Edwardian clothes who demanded to know why they were trespassing on her land. She spoke English with a Scottish accent and was obviously very angry. The three apologised but she continued to complain, adding some bitter comments about modern manners.

A shouted enquiry from the others made the three look round; when they turned back the old lady had vanished. And, it transpired, none of the others had seen her at all.

Local enquiries revealed that, although no eccentric Scottish lady lived there then, the local landowner's great grandfather had married 'the girl from Scotland' at the turn of the century.

Was the figure a curiously talkative ghost? A collective hallucination? Or did the skiers hold a real conversation with a woman from the past – 'the girl from Scotland'?

---

actively involved in some historical occasion. One woman, Mrs D. Dove, while walking near Bootham Bar, York, suddenly found herself in the past when a shaft of sunlight struck a coat of arms on the medieval city gate. At once her awareness of the present dissolved and she discovered herself standing in the midst of a medieval scene; milling barrows, carts and a great crowd of people. She saw mounted horsemen clearing the way for some great personage who followed them. Then the Sun went in and the whole glowing picture disappeared. There seems little doubt that Mrs Dove 'saw' an actual historical scene and was herself briefly a part of it; much as Mrs Turrell-Clarke of Pyrford found herself in the role of a nun in 13th-century Surrey (see page 87).

Here again the trigger factor is present; in this case the sudden shaft of light on the coat of arms on the city gate. Is it possible that the Bar itself had 'recorded' this scene from its own past, and that the particular conditions of light provided by the sudden flash of sunshine 'switched on' the 'playback'? If that were so, why did the Bar 'choose' to replay this scene out of all its millions of recorded moments? And why was the scene not witnessed and reported by everyone else present in the modern precincts of Bootham Bar in 20th-century York? Perhaps that particular scene had some special significance for Mrs Dove, such as a spontaneous memory of a past life? Or perhaps her brain alone was in the necessary state to receive the information and transform it into pictures and sound.

Tuning in to time

The human brain operates electrically and uses several frequencies. There is some variation from brain to brain, and not all operate on exactly the same frequencies. It is possible that persons sensitive to psychic phenomena are merely tuning in to existing wave patterns (either past or future) by accident, their own brain activity being on the correct frequency for reception at the time. Tom Lethbridge, the master dowser, reached much the same conclusion.

It is also true that many bizarre time

Above: Bootham Bar, one of York's medieval city gates, where Mrs Dove experienced a slip back into the city's past when a sudden shaft of sunlight struck a coat of arms on the Bar. Was the sunlight a trigger that somehow 'replayed' a real historical scene?

experiences can be explained as hallucinations. The brain's memory processes are incompletely understood, and the subconscious mind has proved to be very complex; dreams and hypnosis reveal a level of creativity inaccessible to the conscious mind. And the full scope of genetic inheritance is not yet known. Time dislocations may sometimes be the result of these or of imaginative responses, forms of hysteria, drug usage or illness. However, when all these factors have been considered and eliminated, there remains a great number of experiences that cannot be accounted for – or can only be accounted for by analogies that relate to the electromagnetic force field every human possesses, and through which he doubtless gives and receives information. If electrical data fed into the brain from outside sources is capable of being translated by that brain into terms of pictures and sound, then many so-called psychic phenomena, including timeslips, may be explained.

Index